The Mysteries of Modern London

George R. Sims

Alpha Editions

This edition published in 2024

ISBN : 9789361477560

Design and Setting By
Alpha Editions
www.alphaedis.com
Email - info@alphaedis.com

As per information held with us this book is in Public Domain.
This book is a reproduction of an important historical work. Alpha Editions uses the best technology to reproduce historical work in the same manner it was first published to preserve its original nature. Any marks or number seen are left intentionally to preserve its true form.

Contents

CHAPTER I A NOTE OF INTRODUCTION—WHERE WE SHALL GO AND WHAT WE SHALL SEE ....- 1 -
CHAPTER II BY THE WATERSIDE ....- 8 -
CHAPTER III AT THE FASHIONABLE HOTEL ....- 15 -
CHAPTER IV IN A COMMON LODGING-HOUSE.........- 23 -
CHAPTER V THE WAYS OF CRIME ....- 31 -
CHAPTER VI IN THE CITY OF REFUGE ....- 39 -
CHAPTER VII BEHIND THE SCENES ....- 46 -
CHAPTER VIII THE HOUSES OF TRAGEDY ....- 53 -
CHAPTER IX LUNATICS AT LARGE ....- 60 -
CHAPTER X "FROM INFORMATION RECEIVED" ....- 67 -
CHAPTER XI THE MYSTERY OF MONEY SPENT ....- 74 -
CHAPTER XII THE UNKNOWN FATE ....- 81 -
CHAPTER XIII THE FAMILY SKELETON.......................- 89 -
CHAPTER XIV THE ROMANCE OF POVERTY ....- 96 -
CHAPTER XV THE GARDEN OF GUILT ....- 104 -
CHAPTER XVI THE BLACK SHEEP...............................- 110 -
CHAPTER XVII CHILDREN AND CRIME ....- 117 -
CHAPTER XVIII BEHIND BRICK WALLS ....- 123 -
CHAPTER XIX THE SOCIAL MASK ....- 129 -
CHAPTER XX. THE SINS OF THE FATHERS ....- 135 -
CHAPTER XXI. THE ROMANCE OF REALITY ....- 142 -
CHAPTER XXII. SOME CONTRASTS ....- 149 -
CHAPTER XXIII. AT DEAD OF NIGHT..........................- 157 -
CHAPTER XXIV THE UNDIVULGED SECRET ....- 164 -

CHAPTER I
A NOTE OF INTRODUCTION—WHERE WE SHALL GO AND WHAT WE SHALL SEE

Unrecorded crimes—The mystery of the grave—The fascination of the unknown—The shady friends we make—The romance of the railway carriage—Who and what is your neighbour?—How I find my way about

A MYSTERY is, in a popular sense, that which cannot be easily explained; a circumstance that cannot be readily accounted for. Something is, but how or why we cannot tell. The mysteries of modern London are as the sands of the seashore. The mighty city itself is a mystery. The lives of thousands of its inhabitants are mysteries. In the glare and clamour of the noonday, as in the darkness and silence of the night, the mysteries arise, sometimes to startle the world, sometimes to attract so little attention that the story of them never reaches the public ear.

There are mysteries blazoned forth with all the glamour that the contents-bill and the headline can give them, and there are mysteries that are jealously guarded by those high in authority, lest public curiosity should seek to fathom them.

There are mysteries in splendid mansions and in squalid garrets which contain all the elements of criminal romance, and yet pass with the police and the press as matter-of-fact incidents of London's daily life.

The great river hides more mysteries than ever the Seine gave up to the Paris Morgue, and many of them end with a little rest in a quiet mortuary, a "found drowned" hand-bill posted for a day or two on a police-station notice-board, an inquest, an open verdict, and a pauper's funeral.

But among the victims have been men and women the story of whose doing to death would have thrilled the masses and the classes alike; in some instances would have revealed the presence in our midst of active agents of the most desperate secret societies in the world.

There are no mysteries of modern London more terrible than its unrecorded ones. There are disappearances that are never chronicled; murders that are never discovered; victims of foul play who go certified to the grave as having succumbed to "natural causes."

If it were realized that scores of people whose death has been accomplished by the hand of the assassin are quietly buried in London cemeteries every year without the slightest suspicion of wrong, the public would be startled. But the fact remains. And its most convincing illustration is that in almost every case where a poisoner has been tried, the exhumation of former wives or relatives who have died in circumstances which the latest revelation makes suspicious, has proved that they were poisoned too.

Fire has its mysteries, which are rarely revealed. Arson is not entirely practised for the sake of the insurance-money. It happens sometimes that there is loss of life. A house has ere now been burnt to the ground to conceal a crime or to secure a death. The murderer makes good his own escape; the victim is found when at last the brave firemen are able to search among the smoking ruins.

The story of "Enoch Arden" is told again and again in our public journals, sometimes with all the pathetic romance that the Laureate wove into his poem, sometimes with the sordid details of threats and blackmail.

But all the husbands and the wives who part and go their separate ways, forget each other and contract other alliances, do not make the circumstances of their chance re-encountering public.

The tragedy has happened ere now in the stalls of a theatre, in a crowded ball-room, in a fashionable restaurant. The supposed dead man has looked carelessly across the room and seen a woman go-white as death as her eyes met his. She has explained to the husband sitting by her side that it was a sudden faintness, and from that hour has had a terror in her heart that has spoilt her life.

There sits in the House of Lords to-day a statesman whose ancestor, following his wife to the grave, met in the churchyard a stranger who had also come to pay the last respect to a dead wife. A strange story was told, and the two husbands stood side by side at the grave, both mourning the same woman.

As it happened then, so it happened in recent years in a great London cemetery. The death of a well-known man appeared in the papers, and in the announcement was the place of interment and the hour of the ceremony.

The widow laid her cross of lilies reverently on the coffin as it was lowered, and turned weeping away; then through the crowd came a woman closely veiled and when the coffin had been lowered dropped upon the lid a little bunch of violets.

She had left her husband for fifteen years and made no sign, and he had married again. But she read of his death in the country town where she was living, and came to the cemetery.

No one in the crowd of mourners knew the truth, but the younger widow learnt it afterwards in some mysterious way, and in her perplexity let her husband's relatives know of her discovery. And because of the lawsuit they brought with regard to the will the truth became known.

The mysteries of crime and of wrong-doing are common to all cities and to all races. They are part and parcel of the history of civilization. It is not my object in these pages to bring out the sensational features of police romance. My desire is to act as a guide to those who would look beneath the surface of life in the world's great capital, who would wander about its highways and by-ways and see with me that which lies hidden from the casual observer. If I can help my readers to see behind the veil, to peer into the dark recesses, to study out-of-the-way aspects of life as it is lived by thousands of their fellow-citizens, I shall have accomplished a task which has for its object not the gratifying of a morbid curiosity, but the better understanding of things as they are in the great city which is at once the wonder and the admiration of the world.

We shall see life in many of its strangest phases, in its best and sometimes, perhaps, in its worst. We shall take our journeys in search of London's mysteries at all hours of the day, and sometimes in the dead of night, when all good people are supposed to be in bed and asleep, but when thousands are out earning an honest living, and hundreds are abroad to earn a dishonest one.

"How do all these people get money?" is a question which comes naturally to the lips as one gazes at a great crowd of human atoms jostling and elbowing their way along the busy thoroughfares on a working day. And that question puts in a sentence one of the greatest mysteries of modern London.

Alike in the City and in the West there are for ever mixing with the crowd men and women whose means of obtaining a livelihood are mysteries to all but themselves. The tragedies and comedies of life cross each other at every movement of the crowd. The melodrama passes side by side with all that is ordinary and humdrum in the monotony of everyday existence.

In the 'buses and the trams and the trains the silent passengers sit side by side, and no man troubles about his neighbour. But the mysteries of modem London are represented in the crowded vehicle and in the packed compartment. The quiet-looking woman sitting opposite you in the omnibus knows the secret that the police have been seeking to discover for months. The man who politely raises his hat because he touches you as he passes from his seat would, if the truth were known, be standing in the dock of the Old Bailey to answer a capital charge.

The actors and actresses in London's wild romances and terrible tragedies on shoulders with their fellows every day.

I had for months upon my study table the card of a man with the story of whose crime a few months later all England rang. He came to me in the ordinary way about a theatrical matter. He had written a pantomime—I have the book of the words—and he was about to write a comic opera. I chatted with him for a quarter of an hour, bade him good-bye, and forgot all about him until he became the sensation of the day.

He murdered and robbed a fellow-traveller in a railway carriage, made his escape, and was found hiding in a back street London lodging, brought to justice, convicted and executed.

One of the most famous adventuresses of our day, a woman whose whole life had been a romance of daring imposture, left her umbrella in my hall-stand when she drove away in a hansom. She came to claim it a week later. In the meantime she had committed a fraud which later on secured her a long term of penal servitude. It never for a moment in these cases crossed my mind that I was entertaining a man capable of a brutal murder and a woman who was to rank among the celebrated female impostors of the century. To few of us does it occur as we come and go in the course of the day's work or pleasure that we are actually in touch with the mysteries of wickedness and crime.

Going from the Old Bailey not long since, at the conclusion of a murder trial, I got to Farringdon Street just as a train was starting, and scrambled into a third-class carriage. It was nearly full, and I took the last seat. Instantly I recognized two of my fellow-travellers. They were an elderly woman and a young woman, both dressed in deep black.

No one took any notice of them. But what objects of interest they would have been to the other passengers had the identity of one of them been known!

She was the affianced wife of a young man who had that day been condemned to death for the barbarous murder of the woman to whom he was already married. The girl who was sitting with her mother in the crowded compartment on the Metropolitan Railway had just parted with the man who had murdered another woman to make her his wife, and had that day been sent to the gallows.

I had heard this poor girl on the previous day tell in the crowded court one of the strangest incidents of the tragedy. When all London was ringing with the mystery of the murder, her affianced husband came to tea with her people. The talk turned upon the startling crime, and everybody present said they hoped the murderer would soon be discovered. And all the time the murderer was sitting at the tea-table, the honoured guest of that happy little family party!

It is because its mystery has fascinated me from the beginning, and because the spell has never been weakened, that I have wandered London in every direction night and day in a ceaseless endeavour to know it in every phase and form. In these years of wandering, often far off the beaten track, I have learnt much that is not common knowledge, and every day I am learning more. If I were to say that London has laid its heart bare to me it would be untrue, for that has happened to no man. Many of its inner workings are mysteries even to those whose task in life it is to solve them.

But I have penetrated far enough to be able to act as guide to those who have no opportunity of making the journey by themselves, who, even if they had, would make it with small profit to their knowledge of facts.

For the truth does not lie in the open road, and to take the narrow winding way that leads to it, one must be armed with two things—the word that will carry you past the vigilant sentinels and the knowledge that will insure your safe return.

I have said so much that the reader who wishes to accompany me in these journeys in search of the mysterious side of London life may know over what ground we shall have to travel But I should like to say one word more. We shall not need police escort or protection. My obligation to the police is great for many kindly services rendered, and I have the sincerest admiration for the patience and the energy with which they guard the capital's wealth and the lives of its citizens, but I have never asked for their assistance in my journeyings into dark places. The police are known, and in their presence the tongue of the local gossip is tied, and the intentions of the person accompanying them are suspected.

Wherever I have gone it has always been alone or with someone whom the inhabitants of the area—whether honest or criminal, toilers or idlers, decent folk or outcasts—have always regarded with a friendly eye.

Often a journey has been made alone. It has been made by day and by night, and though there have been times when I have been glad to see the beaten track and the lights and the traffic again, I have never received either insult or injury. And I have Been in spots that are officially recognized as the most dangerous in London.

I do not make this statement in any boastful spirit, for there is no credit due to me for escaping the dangers of the dark alley and the underground cellar, the peril of the secret haunt of the foreign desperadoes, the attack of the prowling hooligan, and the wrath of the criminal surprised in the active practice of his profession.

I have gone with a passport which has enabled me to secure, if not the absolute confidence of the victims of my curiosity, at least their abstention from active resistance to my intrusion.

But the mysteries of London do not confine themselves to any one quarter or to any one class. They are to be found in the broad terraces of the West as often as in the narrow alleys of the East. In the criminal courts it is not always the prisoner in the dock who has the ghastliest skeleton in his cupboard. When the police van passes the aristocratic equipage with the coronetted panels, the elegantly dressed occupant of the latter may have the haunting terror of to-morrow in her heart, while the outcast on her road to Holloway is by comparison free from care. There are mysteries in the lordly mansions of the West that make wealth a mockery and rank a disaster. The jealous guarding of the family secret is a task that embitters the lives of brave men and fair women who bear the name that discovery would stain and besmirch.

In London, because it is the capital of the world, are the mysteries of many lands. London is a city of refuge for the outcasts of the Continent. It is an international Alsatia, where the laws from which the alien inhabitants have fled cease to run. There are quiet cafés and restaurants and clubs hidden away in back streets in which men and women meet and eat, drink, dance, and play cards according to their mood, and plot between whiles the deeds that will be ranked with the master crimes of the age. In the dingy lodging-houses of the side streets of Soho the French murderer and murderess may be leading quiet and simple lives while the Parisian police are searching for them through the length and breadth of France. In the Italian quarter that lies off the Gerkenwell Road the agents of the Mafia frequent the little wine-shops and are in constant communication with the heads of the dreaded society in Italy. Here the vendetta that in this country we associate with Italian melodrama and opera is brought to its tragic fulfilment. The stolid London policeman assists at another "stabbing affray" in Little Italy, and is informed that it arose out of a quarrel in a public-house.

But behind that quarrel and the stab or the pistol-shot lies a death-sentence passed months ago in Naples or in Milan, and presently the emissary of vengeance, having accomplished his task, is smuggled out of the country by trusty and tried accomplices, who pay their rent punctually to a London landlord, and draw cheques which are honoured by their London banker.

There are romances of the "Mysterious East," strange and weird, working themselves out behind closed doors and curtained windows in the by-ways of Limehouse and Millwall. There, amid Hindu and Mohammedan rites, deeds are done whose story would read like a page from "The Arabian Nights." There are gloomy dens near the river in which solemn Chinamen, with impassive frees, are engaged in a business which would seem incredible to the Englishman if he read it in a volume that described the mysteries of Pekin.

There are dealers in spells and charms and philtres, and all the stock-in-trade of the witches, the magicians and the sorcerers, carrying on in the centre of London's rush and roar a prosperous trade, not only with the poor and ignorant, but with the rich and cultured. And among all the mysteries of London, few have a deeper or more tragic meaning than those in which the occult and the supernatural play a part.

Not all these mysteries lend themselves to the earnest student who seeks only the truth, who wants to see for himself and to tell a plain unvarnished tale. But many do, and it is these that I shall endeavour to lay before the reader, without sensationalism, without exaggeration, telling a simple story of things as they are.

Facts are more wonderful than fiction, the truth is stranger than any written tale could ever hope to be. I do not propose to dwell on horrors, or to tell again the story of startling crimes. London, the modern Babylon, the Mother of Mysteries, lies before us. It is from her own lips that we will hear the story of much that is strange and mysterious in her life.

CHAPTER II
BY THE WATERSIDE

The River of Death—How the hooligan works—The story of a man who escaped—"Found drowned"—The tragedy of vengeance—The mystery of John Wilson—The woman in the case

A THIN mist wraps London in a shroud of grey this dismal winter afternoon as we pick our path carefully along the miry roads and sodden footways that lead us to the gloomy little building where the mysteries of the quiet water come to the light of day again.

We have come by a region of desolation, across waste land and black patches of marshy earth where men sow seed and dig and wait patiently for a few stunted vegetables to reward their toil. Here and there under the black archways, above which the trains of a great railway thunder and shriek, we have seen a group of pale-faced, scantily-clad urchins kicking a black and battered football about among broken glass and rubbish heaps, and perhaps finding as much joy in the game as the famous performers who make a goal amid the cheers of tens of thousands of spectators.

And so, gradually—always in the mist, always in the mud—we have come to a low-lying, far-stretching expanse of dingy houses and black palings and damp, oozy walls—a bit of Holland, as it were, in which the land and the water meet upon a dead level, and the only reliefs for the wearied eye are the glimmering lights of the barges and the timber ships lying far down the quiet canal.

If we turned off the muddy road and passed inside the black palings we should be by the waterside, and on the broad towing-path that, dotted here and there with lonely little houses and black, mysterious-looking sheds and outbuildings, in the gathering night suggests that river of the nether regions over which the souls of the departed pass.

And to call this silent water-way, glistening darkly where here and there a ray of lamp-light falls upon it, the Styx, would be no wild flight of fancy, for surely to those who know its record this is a River of Death.

The humid, mud-trampled pathways that run on either side are the highways of tragedy—the beaten track of the last footsteps. Here by the water-way that brings the golden freight from the great river to the heart of the busy town is the parting of the ways of Time and Eternity for many a one who lays down the burthen of life.

Not a pleasant place this, on a night of gloom, to linger and look and think. One raises one's eyes from the black water and sees far off the lights of the vehicles that cross the bridges in a steady stream, and the movement of busy life is a relief at once.

Beyond the refuge of despair the world is alive with hope, and the hum of patient toil and the stir of brave endeavour paint us a brighter picture of humanity.

But we have come as students to mark and to learn. We have looked upon the scene of sorrow, where many a tragedy of life comes to its last act. Let us hear the story of some of these tragedies of the water-way that are among the mysteries of modern London.

A few steps from the waterside and we are by a quiet grey church railed off from the road. We pass through a little gateway into a courtyard that leads to a building where those who have sought the waters of forgetfulness rest for a while before they are laid reverently to their last rest.

Not all who come here from the watery depths have taken their own lives. About the tragedies of which the law here seeks to know the truth there is often a mystery that is never penetrated.

Of the three hundred and eighty-six men and women who lay in this hostel of the dead in one year a large number were brought in from the canal. Of these, evidence in thirty-two cases did not, in the opinion of the juries, justify a verdict of suicide. Neither did it justify a verdict of murder, though in many cases the circumstances were more than suspicious.

The ugly wounds might be accounted for by passing barges; but wounding is not, as a rule, part of the process of waterside murder.

The victim is either pushed in in the course of a struggle or first stunned with a blow on the head or garotted, and then thrown in. In the first case there will be no positive signs after a few days' immersion. In the case of garotting there are also difficulties of proof. It is only when there is the mark of the knife or the pistol-shot, or some injury that points conclusively to deliberate infliction, that the worst construction can be placed on the tragedy.

Garotting was the method adopted by the hooligans who at one time infested the canal side, and made it so perilous a place that now the banks are patrolled by plain-clothes officers.

The gangs of young roughs who gather in secluded parts of the banks, where they are hidden by sheds or stacks of material, are there to gamble. They have such a well-organized system of guarding against the unwelcome intrusion of the policeman by well-placed "scouts," that in order to circumvent them it has become necessary to employ detectives for the tow-path.

These disguise themselves in such a way that they can pass without attracting the suspicion of the sentinels posted at a convenient distance from the muddy Monte Carlo. Most of the youths are hooligans of the worst class, and occasionally the little game of pitch-and-toss is only indulged in to reassure the stranger who, coming alone in the gloaming, or at night, might not like the look of the band, and so might take precautionary measures.

On a quiet Sunday afternoon some little time back a young man walking along the path in broad daylight was suddenly set upon by one of these gangs. He escaped the fate intended for him, and lived to tell the tale. He was going to tea with some friends, and was dressed in a frock-coat, and had on a watch and chain and a scarf-pin, and he had some loose silver in his pocket. He came upon a group of young roughs playing cards behind a stack of timber, looked at them, and passed on. It never occurred to him that on a bright Sunday afternoon in the heart of London a man could be robbed and murdered.

But before he had gone half a dozen paces farther he felt his throat clutched from behind, and two powerful hands trying to throttle him. At the same time two roughs seized his arms, while another of the gang took the watch and chain and pin and went over the victim's pockets.

But the victim was a strong young fellow, and fought desperately, though a hand thrust over his mouth prevented him from calling out.

"Throw him in!" exclaimed one of the gang.

There was a desperate struggle on the tow-path. The man, knowing that he would be stunned and pushed into the canal, to be found there perhaps days afterwards and looked upon as a suicide, fought furiously for his life.

He managed by a desperate effort to fling off his assailants, and then he took to his heels and fled. He reached his home in a condition of such exhaustion that there he fainted. The usage he had received was so brutal that he was compelled to keep his bed for a week.

That is the story of a man who escaped. The men, and the women, too, who have been less fortunate in their encounters with waterside assassins have been "found drowned."

It is a remarkable thing that there is hardly ever any money on the bodies that are brought from the canal to the mortuary. Every article found is entered in a book kept for that purpose by the official in charge. If you turn over the pages, you will find against almost every entry in which the word "drowned" occurs the words "no money" also.

To this last Guest House on the road to God's Acre there come again and again the mysteries of the unclaimed dead. Someone lies there waiting to be identified, and waits in vain. Neither kith nor kin come forward. The man has mattered so little to anyone that he has been able to pass out of life without a fellow-creature troubling as to why his home and his accustomed haunts know him no more.

Sometimes the identity of the dead upon whom the curious or the anxious come to gaze is violently disputed. Not long since two women claimed one man as a missing husband, and in the end it was proved that he belonged to neither of them. Yet both recognized the features and the clothes, and both gave certain indications as to marks which were found to exist on the body. Only those who have official knowledge of the number of people who come to identify a body "found drowned" are aware of the vast number of men and women who leave their homes and make no communication to their relatives as to their whereabouts. And these people are not always of the poorest class.

Here lay some time ago a man done to death—a foreigner shot in the streets of London. The man had been tracked by an assassin sent by a secret society from his native land. The society's agent came to London with orders to shoot the condemned man on sight.

Soon after the news of the crime got into the papers, two men of the victim's own nationality came to the mortuary to see if they could identify him.

One glance was sufficient. As they turned shuddering away, one muttered to the other, "This fate is for us, too; we shall be the next." A few days later those men met their doom, and came to lie side by side with the first victim.

The murderer being eventually discovered in the neighbourhood, and brought to bay, shot himself as he was on the point of being arrested. He was brought to this mortuary, too, and made up a gruesome quartette.

This tragedy of vengeance, as thrilling as any story that is told of the Italian Vendetta or the Russian Terrorism, happened in a quiet London suburb. These people lived in modest apartments, without a vestige of romance about them to suggest to the landlady, or the servant girl who waited on them, that they were men whose death-sentence had been pronounced by the committee of a secret society in Eastern Europe, and that one by one they were to fall to the pistol-shot of the man who had drawn the lot which made him their executioner. It reads like a page torn from a wildly sensational story. It happened in a popular London suburb, among the trams and 'buses, the crowded streets and the busy shops.

A portion of the truth was told in the court of the coroner, a good deal that lay behind the tragedy was imagined; but there were elements of mystery in this romance of the East, transplanted to the West, which yet remain to be solved.

Year in, year out, all days of the week, the mysteries of life and death come to this building of sad significance.

At the iron gate that shuts it off from the roadway the mortuary-keeper stood one summer evening. A young workman came along the street whistling. It was the young fellow's wont as he passed every evening on his way home to exchange greeting with the mortuary-keeper if he happened to be at the gate. His greeting was generally a grim joke: "All right, John," he used to say, "I'm not coming in just yet."

This summer evening as he passed he nodded and made his usual joke. "I'm not coming in just yet," he said, and went laughing on his way. He had not gone ten paces before he tottered and fell suddenly to the ground. Almost before the echo of his laughter at his own grim joke had died away, he was carried through the gates.

These are the mysteries of life and death that find their way to the House of Rest by the waterside. They are mysteries perhaps only in the sense that they are phases of the great human drama of which the busy world sees little. We pass our way without a thought of the strange happenings hidden from us by a few thin walls. Upon the mimic stage the fourth wall is always down. On the stage of life it stands and hides from all the working out of the great scheme of things. It is the fourth wall that makes many a mystery over which the world puzzles unexplainable.

There is a mystery in connection with this waterside mortuary for which an explanation has been sought in vain. The story is simple, and yet it has in it all the elements of a modern detective romance.

Just before the Coronation Day that was to have been, a man about fifty, fairly well dressed, came along the side of the canal and looked at the water. It was a broiling hot day, and it was by no means uncommon for people to leave the roadway to take a stroll nearer the cool-looking canal.

The man was seen by passers-by and people who were loitering about, but no idea was entertained that he was going to commit suicide.

Suddenly he flung off his hat and leapt into the water.

The alarm was given. A little crowd gathered on the tow-path and did their best, but failed to rescue the man. It was half an hour before the body was recovered and taken across the road to the mortuary.

The usual careful examination was made, and in the man's breast-pocket was found an envelope on which was written: "I am John Wilson of New York." I am not giving the man's real name. There was no property of any kind found, and nothing else to lead to identification. The usual public announcements were made, and the first discovery was that a man answering the description of the deceased had been to a local firm the evening previous to the suicide, had stated he was a carpenter, and had applied for a job to assist in erecting Coronation seats.

But the foreman who gave this information stated that the man was a complete stranger to him, and only said that he was a carpenter.

The next person who came forward was a lady, apparently in good circumstances. She stated that she had seen a newspaper report, and had no doubt that the man was her brother. Before being allowed to proceed to identification, she was asked for further particulars. She produced a photograph and showed it to the official. The photograph was certainly not that of the dead man, and the official said so.

The lady was sure it must be. The name published as found on the envelope was that of her brother, who had come to this country some little time before from New York. He was not a carpenter, or anything of that sort, and she could not understand how he could have applied for work, unless, as she supposed, his mind had become affected. She had not seen him for some little time.

The photograph not being like the man, the lady was asked, as she was so positive, if she could give any indications which would assist the authorities in accepting her statement.

"Yes," she said. "My brother always had a fear of something happening to him, and lest his papers should be taken from him, he was in the habit of writing his name on a slip of paper and sewing it up in the lining of his waistcoats."

The official went at once to the room in which the clothes were kept locked away, ripped open the lining of the waistcoat, and found inside it a slip of paper, on which was written in the same handwriting as that on the envelope: "I am John Wilson of New York."

There was nothing more to be said. The evidence was accepted as conclusive. The inquest was held, and the lady arranged the funeral.

As she stated that her brother was insured in New York for a large sum of money, and that she was his only relative, and entitled to the insurance, the matter passed into the hands of a firm of solicitors, and the necessary certificates of death and burial were supplied.

There the matter would have ended, so far as the police on this side were concerned, and would probably have been forgotten, but for the startling fact that some months later a communication came from New York which put an extraordinary complexion on the affair.

One of the insurance-offices declined to pay, and advised the solicitor who had acted in England that the person whose certificate had been forwarded was not John Wilson of New York, as John Wilson, the person whose life they had insured, had been found alive, and this John Wilson was the brother of the lady who claimed the insurance-money.

There the matter rests at present, so far as the mortuary authorities are concerned.

If the American statement is correct, then a man who was not John Wilson must have committed suicide with the name of John Wilson not only in his pocket, but with a second clue to identification sewn up in the lining of his clothing. John Wilson's sister had informed the authorities that it was there, and there they had found it.

The man was a carpenter by trade, according to his own last recorded statement. How did he come to sew another man's name in his clothing, and then deliberately commit suicide? Did he personate an insured person to oblige someone else? Or was it one of those extraordinary coincidences of two men of the same name and nationality having the same habit of preparing for identification in case of accident?

The night has fallen ere we pass through the iron gate, which closes behind us with a clang. Here and there a few shadowy figures move about in the mist that rises from the damp ground. In the yellow flicker of a lonely lamp the black palings that shut off the towpath shine with an oily lustre. Beyond, stretching away into the dim distance, the gloomy waters of the canal lie silent and motionless, hiding many a mystery still.

CHAPTER III
AT THE FASHIONABLE HOTEL

Big incomes that do not exist—Visit to a gambling club—A deep-laid plot—Heavy blackmail—A masterly stroke—Two biters bitten

EVERY now and then the world is startled by the story of a woman who has succeeded in obtaining thousands of pounds from men of the world and men of business who have believed in her completely, and have fallen victims to the oldest form of the confidence dodge—a clever woman's own representation that she is entitled to a large fortune, or in possession of property which for the moment she is unable to realize.

You have only to talk "big" enough to find plenty of people prepared to take you at your own valuation. The adventurer who wants to live luxuriously on his wits does not proceed on quite the same lines as the adventuress. In some respects his is a harder task, in others it is an easier one.

London swarms with men and women of all grades, whose sole means of livelihood is the credulity of the people with whom they come in contact.

The footman who persuades the lady of rank that he is a prince, and the loafer who engages himself to half a dozen servant girls a month in order to get money and their bits of jewellery, pursue practically the same methods. They go through a process which in the sporting circles is known as "telling the tale." Given a certain amount of tact and a veneer of culture, and men or women who set out deliberately to do so can assume any rank or position they consider best for the particular fraud they have in hand.

There are plenty of people in London to-day whose legitimate income is under £100 a year, and who yet live in well-appointed houses in good neighbourhoods, keep servants, and entertain on a lavish scale. In the great London hotels there are always a number of guests who are nothing but adventurers and adventuresses.

The well-dressed, well-mannered "dangerous class" has increased rapidly of late years. The conditions of modern life are wholly favourable to its development. The breaking down of social barriers which has marked the new century has opened up new and profitable fields of enterprise. In a day when millionaires spring up like mushrooms, and anybody with an American accent or a Jewish name is accepted as fabulously rich "without further inquiry," it is the easiest thing in the world for the skilful adventurer to work himself into any society—even to obtain the entrée to houses where, once having been seen, his reputation is hall-marked.

No one, as a rule—except a tradesman swindled out of his goods—seeks to pry into the mystery of these people's means. The source of the incomes of so many who live luxuriously today is a mystery, that suspicion has been lulled, and anyone with a few pounds and a portmanteau or a Saratoga trunk has only to put up a well-frequented London hotel to start making a useful circle of acquaintances at once.

Some of these people are known to the police. Their record is at Scotland Yard. It is this fact that occasionally leads to the occupant of an elegant apartment being presented with his or her bill by the management, and at the same time a polite intimation that their room is required for another guest who has secured it for that date. Sometimes the person so treated argues the matter out with a show of indignation. But, as a rule, discretion is considered the best part of valour, and the agreeable Mr. So-and-So or the charming Mrs. So-and-So is missed from the lounge or the smoking-room or the drawingroom, and the departure regretted. For these people are always "nice." If they were not, they would make no friends, and it is by the making of friends they live.

But more frequently the hotel adventurer and adventuress have not come under the official notice of the detective police. The men of position who are swindled by women, the women of good social standing who are duped by men, do not care to advertise their simplicity to the world. It is on this distaste for publicity on the part of their victims that high-class adventurers and adventuresses rely.

At a fashionable London hotel some time ago a young American arrived. He bore a well-known name, and was a partner in his father's business. The wealth and position of his family were discussed in the smoking-room, one or two Americans present volunteering information to an Englishman who had started the topic of conversation.

This Englishman, satisfied as to the *bona fides* of the newcomer, lost no time in making his acquaintance, and very obligingly "showed him London"—the side of it which is not in the guide-books. One night the young American was taken by his friend to a club in a side street in Soho, which he was told was a gambling club. He need not play, but the company were worth seeing. The young fellow did not want to play, but was quite willing to look on. All of a sudden a dispute arose among the players—there were about a dozen, among them some foreigners—there was a scuffle, one of the foreigners whipped out a dagger and plunged it into the breast of a man with whom he was quarrelling, his victim fell to the ground, the lights were turned down, and as the company made a rush to the door the police entered.

"This way," said the Englishman to his friend, and dragged him through a little door in the back of the room into a kitchen, out into a passage, and up a court into the main street, where they hailed a hansom and drove back to the hotel.

"We've had a narrow escape," said the Englishman. "It would have been pretty hard if we had been walked off to the station and charged. Of course, that club's illegal, and this stabbing business will be bad for everybody who was there." The young American was very thankful to have escaped the unpleasantness.

In an evening paper the next day appeared a mysterious paragraph. A man had been found stabbed in a gambling houses The police had arrested several persons present, but it was stated by the victim, who was in a precarious condition, that he believed his assailant was a young American, who managed to escape after the police had entered. The proprietor of the establishment, who was in custody, had given information which, it was hoped, would lead to the identification of the assassin. The American was horrified.

"But you know this is absurd," he said to his English friend, who gave him the paper to read. "You saw the foreigner do it." The Englishman shook his head. "It's a nasty business," he said, "and unpleasant for both of us. It's evident that the proprietor and the other people are in league to save the real culprit."

"But the man who was stabbed—he must know who did it?"

"He thinks he'll get well, I suppose, and he's afraid of accusing the real man. Some of these people belong to the most dangerous gang in London. They'll put the thing on you because they think you're not likely to come forward and deny it."

"Say," said the American, "I don't like this—it looks bad. I shall leave here and go to Paris. I wouldn't get mixed up in this business for a thousand. It would be in all the American papers."

The Englishman said he thought the plan a wise one. He himself should go to some friends in the North of England, and keep out of the way for a bit. But the plan was not quite so easily carried out. The friends had been talking together in the courtyard. As they turned to enter the hotel a man came up and touched the American on the shoulder.

"You'll excuse me," he said, "but I saw you two gentlemen at that club where the man was stabbed last night." The two friends looked at each other. Neither knew what to say.

"I was a waiter there," said the man. "I got away just after you by the back door, and followed you up the court. I saw you get into a cab, and I heard you tell the man to drive to this hotel. I thought I'd come and see if I could find you."

The Englishman had recovered himself.

"Look here," he said, "you'd better come up to my friend's room and talk the matter over."

The result of the discussion was that the young American gave the man £300 to keep quiet. He explained that he was a stranger seeing London. He was absolutely innocent of any share in the quarrel, but he didn't want to be detained in London to answer a charge which, absurd as it was, would be a very unpleasant public ordeal.

The Englishman also drew a cheque for £300, and gave it to the man not to drag him into the affair.

The American left London, thinking he had heard the last of the affair. But when he got back to his home in the States he found a letter waiting for him. That waiter had found out who he was, and wanted more hush-money. He wanted $5000. The victim of the attack at the gaming house had died, the writer said, and unless he received the amount named he should communicate with the police. Even if the young-man evaded arrest, the story would be in all the English papers, and copied into the American ones.

The young American read the letter carefully two or three times, and then went to a solicitor, telling him the whole story. The solicitor advised him not to reply, but to let him communicate with an agent in London, who would inquire into the whole affair. The investigation made by the London agent revealed the fact that the police of London were totally ignorant of any such affair, that no one had been found stabbed in a gambling house, and that no police raid on a gambling house in Soho had taken place at that date.

The American visitor to London had been marked down by one of the gang of bad characters who infest hotels for the purpose of swindling strangers. The agreeable Englishman was the concocter of the whole scheme.

The only thing that was a mystery now was the stabbing. The American had seen the dagger plunged into the man's breast.

The stabbing was a comedy, though it had looked like a tragedy at the time. The dagger was a stage dagger, which appears to penetrate the body of the victim, but really goes up the handle. The two policemen who came in were probably made up on the premises for the occasion, and the "gamblers" were members of the gang of blackmailers to which the Englishman staying at the hotel belonged.

It is not likely that this sensational little scene was arranged for the occasion only. It had doubtless been effectually played many times before on unsuspecting visitors to the metropolis. Without the stabbing' it is common enough. One of the commonest tricks of a well-known gang is to lure a visitor anxious to see life to some questionable haunt, and make him the victim of a bogus police raid. The staid and sober citizens of good repute will generally pay handsomely to avoid publicity.

In the case of the young American, a deliberate scheme of lifelong blackmail was planned. The report in the evening newspaper was a master stroke. But there are means of getting a sensational statement that has not a word of truth in it past the most vigilant of sub-editors.

Some of the most dangerous female swindlers in the world are to be found in fashionable hotels. They frequently have foreign titles. Princesses, marchionesses, countesses, and baronesses there are who are well known to the international police, and who yet continue to live luxuriously year in, year out, on a methodical system of fraud.

Few of them are young—many of them are middle-aged, and some are elderly. But they rarely fail to pay their expenses, though they may fail to pay the tradespeople they honour with their patronage. Even in this matter, however, they are careful, and avoid, if they possibly can, any transaction with a shopkeeper which might lead to the publicity of the police court A charge of swindling would be inconvenient. It would necessitate the adoption of a new title, and that would be awkward, because the majority of these adventuresses are too well known to certain people in fashionable resorts to be able to change a title without exciting suspicion.

One of the most brilliant adventuresses of recent years posed as a philanthropist, and visited town after town in furtherance of her philanthropic scheme. She was received with open arms by clergymen, and on two occasions was entertained by local mayors. She might have gone on posing as a philanthropist looking about for a deserving charity on which to bestow a vast sum of money, if she had not allowed herself the indiscretion of falling in love with and marrying a young man who was supposed to be the son of an English nobleman. It was when the police got on the track of the Hon. Mr. Dash, eldest son of Lord Fourstars, and made a descent upon his rooms at a fashionable hotel, that one of the detectives was struck by the resemblance the Hon. Mrs. Dash bore to a woman who had been through his hands some years previously.

The astonishment of the newly married couple, who were on their honeymoon, was not so much at the arrest as at the discovery that they had both deceived each other. In the lady's case the force of the blow was somewhat mitigated by the fact that she had not really lost a title. She had a previous husband somewhere in the colonies.

Both these swindlers met each other first at a fashionable hotel in London. There was some excuse for the man being taken in. When he met the lady she was in the company of a colonial bishop and his wife, with whom she had established quite a friendly intimacy.

With one dangerous type of hotel adventuress—the lady with a husband who arrives unexpectedly and late at night from America—I need not deal. But good round sums have been parted with again and again by quite innocent victims to avoid a scandal. It is at the hotel that the wonderful tale is frequently told which never seems to fail to find victims. It is the story of the fortune that is coming. The idea of great expectations appeals at once to the cupidity of certain natures.

I know at the present moment a simple-minded couple who have as their guest in their pretty country home a young lady who came to stay a week, and has already stayed three months. The parties met at a London hotel. The young lady made the acquaintance of the country couple, and gradually took them into her confidence. She was the niece of a wealthy Australian, an elderly widower, who had died in London without a will.

Her mother was the Australian's only sister, and he had no other relatives. Something like a million of money was involved. On the news of his death reaching Melbourne, the young lady—her mother being in ill-health—had come to London to claim the fortune.

The reader will guess the end of the story. It is as old as the hills. Every now and then it is told in the police court, but as a rule it continues to impose upon its dupes until the impostor has got all that is to be had, and conveniently disappears.

The plot is simple. There are trouble and expense. The available funds have run low, and unless a remittance arrives from somewhere a very long way off, the legal process of claiming the fortune will be delayed. The delay is dangerous. Another claimant who has no earthly right has turned up, and, having money, is forging ahead. A million may be lost for a hundred pounds or so of ready money. The dupes, encouraged by the promise of a bounteous gift when the fortune has been secured, find that hundred or so.

Then a further difficulty occurs. Lawyers' letters, sometimes deeds, are shown, and the victims are bled afresh. To save the loss of the hundred pounds parted with, hundreds more are advanced. Sometimes the bubble bursts in a few weeks. Sometimes it remains floating gracefully for a couple of years.

The people I know have advanced five hundred pounds, and the young lady is still their honoured guest. They refuse to have their faith shaken in her, or to request her to find hospitality elsewhere. They cling to their belief in the plausible adventuress. To acknowledge to themselves that they had been duped would mean to recognize that they had lost five hundred pounds. Human nature is always human nature, and hope springs eternal in the human breast. It is the hope of ultimate success that causes millions of good money to be flung after bad, and keeps the Bankruptcy Court busy.

A mystery that still remains unravelled had its first scene in a London hotel. A young man of fortune, an inebriate, was staying in one. There he met two young men of apparently good social position who were just starting for a European trip.

These men fired the imagination of their new acquaintance. He had better come with them.

The young man consented, informed his friends and his solicitor of his intention, and started, taking with him letters of credit for a large amount.

Two or three communications were received from him from various parts of the Continent. The last letter was from a small Spanish town. After that he only telegraphed when he wanted more money sent out.

He telegraphed from a Spanish sea-coast town for such a large sum of money to be sent, that the solicitor who had charge of his affairs felt it his duty to consult a relative with whom the young man was not friendly, but who was his next-of-kin.

A suspicion seems to have crossed the minds of both that something was wrong, and the British Consul in the town was communicated with. He went to the hotel to which the money was to be sent, and having been supplied with a photograph of Mr. ——— by the solicitor, asked to see him.

The proprietor of the hotel recognized the portrait, said

Mr. ——— was staying there, but was out with two friends.

That evening when the consul called again he saw the two friends. They appeared to be very distressed. They stated that Mr. ——— had been drinking heavily. While out together walking by the shore he had suddenly left them and disappeared. They had made every effort to find him, but had failed, and they feared he must have made his way to a lonely part of the coast and drowned himself.

That was the last that was ever heard of the missing young man who went travelling with two strangers he met at a London hotel.

Whether they would have taken possession of the money had it been sent it was impossible to say. And there was no proof forthcoming that they had anything to do with the disappearance of Mr. ———, though there is very little doubt they had the bulk of the large sum of money he took with him.

There is one feature of the fashionable hotel which is not strictly confined to those who live in it. That is the use made by swindlers of the stamped hotel paper. Thomas, the man who committed the crimes for which the unfortunate Mr. Beck suffered so cruelly, wrote nearly all his letters on the note-paper of fashionable hotels. He simply walked in, sat down at a writing-table, and had at once a good address with which to inspire his victims with confidence.

On the strength of that hotel note-paper he was accepted by experienced women of the world as an English nobleman of vast fortune. The fashionable hotel is the happy hunting ground of the most dangerous criminals known and unknown to the police.

CHAPTER IV
IN A COMMON LODGING-HOUSE

A superior place—Class distinctions—The men who have fallen—The family outcast—The shabby minister—A strange disappearance—The common kitchen

IT is eleven o'clock on Sunday morning, and the church bells have just ceased ringing. Along the broad thoroughfare which is one of the main arteries of London a few belated worshippers are wending their way, prayer-book in hand. But from the side streets come the roar and clamour of a busy market at its height. The hoarse shrieks of the hawkers and the cheap Jacks rise above the murmur of the mob, which elbows its way, a black stream of humanity, between two banks of barrows and open shops.

At the corner of one of the side streets—the corner at which the clamour of the market ends and the quiet of the English Sabbath begins—there is a huge, well-ordered, common lodging-house.

The whole neighbourhood is Jewish, the area is given up now almost entirely to the alien immigrant; but in this vast lodging-house the guests are not Jews but Gentiles.

In the entrance hall there is a case in which the letters awaiting the arrival of guests are exposed. There are letters from abroad, letters with American and colonial stamps on them; envelopes directed in a clerkly hand, envelopes directed in handwriting which tells of culture and refinement, and there are envelopes with a scrawled, ill-spelt address upon them.

For this Hotel of the Poor, where the prices range from five-pence to sixpence a night, has a reputation for comfort, good order, and good management, and attracts a superior order of men to that found in the fourpenny lodging-houses in the locality which are largely patronized by the criminal and the vagabond class.

On Sunday morning the clients of the doss-house lie later. It is a privilege accorded by custom. On ordinary days the guests are expected to be out of bed and downstairs by ten at the latest, but on Sunday, if you go over the dormitories and cubicles, even as late as twelve o'clock, you will find plenty of beds still occupied by slumbering—sometimes by snoring—citizens.

But by noon the majority of the patrons of the Poor Man's Hotel have "descended." Some are lounging against the wall in the street, taking the air. Many are in the vast underground apartment which serves the purpose of a common kitchen, and breakfast is in the course of preparation or consumption. Hard by this apartment is another, which is fitted up with every arrangement for as much ablution as the client of the house may care to indulge in. He can have a bath, or he can wash his face and hands. He can, if he is so minded, brush his hat, and there is a bit of looking-glass, in front of which he can arrange his collar—if he has one—and his necktie.

Fivepence carries you considerably further on the road to comfort here than fourpence does in most of the smaller establishments.

I know the doss-houses of most parts of London. I have spent mornings and evenings round the coke fire of the common kitchen with all sorts and conditions of male and female dossers, and I have always been struck by the note of classification which distinguishes them. Even the poorest of the poor have their sympathies, and, if I may use the word, their "aloofnesses."

The thieves do not care to mix with the honest folks; the tramps and vagabonds look down upon the workers, and the men of the working-class look askance at the wreckage of the black coat brigade. So each class has its own particular doss-houses. Even the begging-letter writers have their favourite haunts; in one house the clients are nearly all begging-letter writers, and sometimes pool the receipts.

The "screever," who is practically a public writer at the service of anyone willing to pay for a well-concocted story and a touching appeal, is not so particular. He puts up at any house where he is likely to find clients.

The lodging-house we are visiting this Sunday morning is so huge, and its accommodation is so vast, that it is patronized by the poor of every class. The poor working man is there, and the poor clerk; the wreckage of the superior class is there also, but there are no professional tramps. The professional tramp would find the society slow, and there would be no one with whom he could compare notes and yarn about the bad times that had come to the road. He prefers the more genial and instructive society of the street beggar, the itinerant musicians, and the "dodgers."

You will rarely see any work being done in a tramps' lodging-house.

The nearest approach to it is when one or two of the company patch their rags or take a needle and thread and collect their rents—those in their garments.

But in the lodging-house we are visiting you will find a number of the occupants hard at work, even on Sunday morning.

Beyond the common kitchen is a room with a long, wide table. Every seat at this table is occupied by men who are writing as diligently as if they were in an office.

Most of the men are of the broken-down clerk class. Many are young; only one or two are middle-aged. But all are lean and dilapidated and hungry-looking.

These poor fellows are addressing envelopes at so much a thousand, or filling in circulars, or doing copying work. On the table is a Post Office Directory for the use of the envelope-directors, and there is a good supply of inkstands.

Some of the men have been at work since nine, and, with a short interval, will work away till late in the afternoon, perhaps till the evening. They are earning the price of the next night's bed.

These men belong to the shabby-genteel brigade of the common lodging-house. Many of them have still the traces of refinement on their features, though their clothes are threadbare and their bowler hats weather-beaten and greasy-brimmed.

Who are they? What stroke of evil fortune brought them to this last ditch in the fight with Fate?

Many of them are mysteries. They do not, like the tramps and the vagabonds, wear their heart upon their sleeve. There is no confidence between them and the other occupants of the "writing-room" in the poor man's hotel.

Some of them have held good positions in mercantile offices and lost them. One or two are lawyers' clerks with whom the world has gone wrong. A fair percentage have come to envelope-directing in a common lodging-house through drink, others through an act that has caused them to forfeit the character essential for a re-engagement. Some of them owe their downfall to the turf. One or two have a conviction standing against them, and that is the sort of thing that stands against you till the last. All have wandered or stumbled into the slough from which few ever emerge to gain a foothold again upon firm ground.

In this room, in which a score of well-educated men are writing hard all Sunday long to get a few coppers, the stragglers of a doomed legion are really making the last stand. They may fight desperately, and hold their ground for a time, but they will yield eventually, and the hospital or the workhouse will claim them.

Yet some of them have homes they have forfeited, wives and children from whom by their own act they have separated themselves for ever.

Among the men I have met in a common lodging-house is one who, every now and then, is interviewed in the common kitchen by his family solicitor. He is a trustee to a marriage settlement, and his signature is occasionally necessary to deeds and transfers. A little while back he had to put his signature to a cheque for £72,000. Why, under these circumstances, is there no home for him—no position open to him in which at least he could earn the rent of a private lodging?

That is a mystery the solution of which is known only to himself, his relatives, and the family solicitor. He has a wife and sons and daughters, and they live in a pretty villa and keep servants, entertain, and visit their neighbours.

But many a night since the thing happened that made it impossible for him ever again to be seen with his own people he has been too poor even to afford the few pence for a doss-house bed, and has had to seek shelter in one of the night refuges for the utterly destitute or sleep under a railway arch.

If we were to stand at the entrance of a lodging-house such as this for a night and watch the guests as they come in—some of them so late that on the outside lamp is the reassuring notice, "A Night Porter kept"—we should see a strange procession of human documents.

If we knew the story of each we should have the details of life romances far more dramatic and haunting than those which are the stock-in-trade of fictionists who sit at home at ease and imagine things.

Look at this man, for instance, who is limping in and cringing to the deputy. If you are in the kitchen to-morrow morning you will see him do the same to a sturdy fellow who enters jauntily. You will see him take a teapot from the hob, where he has been keeping it hot, and put it on the table before the new arrival. The one man is the valet of the other. For a copper or two a week he cleans the other man's boots and gets his breakfast ready.

The man who employs a valet is a professional beggar. He can pitch a good tale, and his features suggest better days, and so he does exceedingly well in certain neighbourhoods. The valet is a mystery. No one knows how he earns his living. Occasionally he leaves the lodging-house for some weeks, saying that he has come into a little money. But he drifts back again, and is generally—if possible—more dilapidated than when he left.

If we were to go to one of the fashionable churches of London to listen to a preacher whose name is a household word, we should be struck with the likeness of that distinguished divine to the lodging-house valet. The likeness is accounted for by the fact that they are brothers. Both were at Harrow, both were at Oxford. But one this Sunday morning is preaching to a wealthy West End congregation, and is on the straight road to a bishopric, while the other is "valeting" a beggar in a common lodging-house.

Clergymen themselves come here sometimes. There is one who comes constantly—generally late at night. He has a cubicle, for which he pays sixpence. However late he may come in, he generally leaves early, before most of the lodgers are about.

He never enters the common kitchen. Sometimes he is shabby and down at heel. Sometimes he appears to have had a little luck, and his appearance is neater. Why a clergyman reduced to using a common lodging-house should retain the distinguished marks of clerical attire it is difficult to say. The deputy is the only person who has had an opportunity of studying him closely. The deputy, who is an excellent judge of character, thinks that the clerical get-up is a dodge; that the man is an impostor. But the proprietor, who, on two occasions, has spoken with his guest, is certain that there is no imposture—that the man is a Clerk in Holy Orders who has come upon evil times. He has been using the lodging-house off and on for the past five years.

Once in the rack at the door there was a letter for him. The envelope had a black border, and was addressed simply "Mr. William Venn."

Letters at the lodging-house are not given to the first person who claims them. Unless a guest is thoroughly well known he is expected to give some proof that he is the person named on the envelope.

In this instance Mr. Venn produced a couple of letters from his pocket. Both were addressed to the Rev. William Venn—I am not giving the correct name—at the General Post Office, "to be called for."

When he came to the lodging-house again there was a black band round the dilapidated high hat he always wore.

He only came back once after he was in mourning. No one at the lodging-house saw him again for some time. Shortly afterwards a solicitor's clerk came to make inquiries. His firm were particularly anxious to find the Rev. William Venn, who was entitled to a considerable sum of money by the death of a relative. The last known address of the reverend gentleman was this lodging-house, to which a relative had sent him the news of his wife's death in a lunatic asylum.

The proprietor took the address of the solicitors, and promised to communicate with them should the clergyman come again.

A year afterwards the clergyman did come—more wretched-looking, more woe-begone than ever.

When he applied for a bed, the deputy at once communicated the good news to him. "There's been somebody here asking for you," he said; "some solicitors. We were to communicate with them if we saw you again. They want you for——"

Before the deputy could finish the sentence the clergyman had fled.

The proprietor of the lodging-house, interested in the case, made several inquiries of the solicitors; but from that night the Rev. William Venn was never seen again.

There is a street in the East End which, owing to the character of its fourpenny lodging-houses, has become notorious. You may see standing at the doors of these houses men and women whose appearance, even in the broad daylight, would make a stranger doubtful as to the advisability of passing near them.

Night after night these houses are crowded with vagabonds, male and female, of the most dangerous type. In one of these, three murders took place in one year.

Nearly every woman who comes out of them has a black eye or some facial disfigurement due to male violence. The younger men have "ruffian" writ large upon their features, while the older men are of the ragged, weather-beaten tramp order.

To spend an evening in the common kitchens is to get an idea of humanity which revolts rather than saddens. Horrifying as the ordinary language of the company is, their callous viciousness and criminality are more horrifying still. There are men here who have taken human life—taken it brutally on dark nights in country lanes and by the waterside, sometimes to rob their victim, sometimes to get rid of a man or woman who knows too much or who wants too much.

Some of the men and women sitting together and indulging in drunken chaff or maudlin reminiscences are old acquaintances. They have met in more than one lodging-house in London, and have tramped together to fairs and race-meetings. And the mildest form of "ragging" among them is to remind each other of the robbery or the outrage, it may be the murder, with which the gossip of the doss-houses credits them.

The one offence which among these people is considered discreditable, and which makes them unfit for the society of their fellows, is to give information to the police, or to give evidence which assists the police in obtaining a conviction.

The man who is suspected of having murdered his wife or his companion is rather looked up to. But the man who has assisted in bringing a murderer to justice is despised, and if he were to return to one of these doss-houses at a time that anyone was present who knew of his conduct, he would have a poor chance of getting out again with a whole skin.

But these people, ragged, dirty, wretched as their appearance generally is, are not always without means. I have been in one of the lowest of these houses on a Sunday morning, when the place was packed, and seen the tramps and beggars enjoying a breakfast that seldom falls to the lot of a poor working family.

Look in at one of the kitchens to-day. Tea with bread and butter, bacon, haddocks, bloaters, and cold fried fish are among the breakfast "relishes" on the table, and in a frying-pan on the fire one stalwart tramp is cooking himself a pork chop.

The man's wallet stowed away on a shelf in the kitchen contains nothing but a few old rags and bits of rubbish picked up by the wayside. But he makes enough somehow to pay for his night's lodging and a good meat breakfast, and you will see him, as soon as the public-house at the corner opens, investing more money in the purchase of a stimulant to assist the digestion of the pork chop. There is always a public-house near a doss-house, and it is liberally patronized by the lodgers.

With all their apparent poverty they find money to visit the gin-palace two or three times in the course of as many hours.

I have seen the same group of women from a notorious doss-house go into a public-house four times in an hour. Two of them were miserably clad, and limped painfully in boots that scarcely held together.

If it is astonishing that men and women who have so much money to spend in drink can put up with the shelter of the lowest of the common lodging-houses in London, it is still more astonishing that men, and sometimes women, of wealth should habitually resort to them.

Yet in a doss-house in Bangor Street, Notting Dale, a woman lodged regularly, who, at the time of her death, had standing to her credit at a local bank several hundred pounds, In a fourpenny lodging-house in Great Peter Street, Westminster, a man who was taken ill and removed to a hospital was found to have upon him a money-belt which contained bank-notes to the value of sixty pounds. In a lodging-house in the Mint—one of a better kind, run in connection with a temperance mission, the lodging-house, in fact, in the kitchen of which the first free meals provided by the "Referee" Children's Dinner Fund were prepared—a man died who was supposed to be almost destitute; so poor and miserable was he, that his bed was paid for every week by a kindly clergyman interested in the mission.

This old fellow used to go to Covent Garden in the morning, pick up vegetable refuse, and bring it back with him and make soup of it. He picked up something one day that made him seriously ill. He was taken to the hospital, and died there, and in the battered old box which he left behind him at the lodging-house were discovered securities for a very large sum of money, and a banker's pass-book with all the entries on the credit side, and not a single one on the debit side.

The mysteries of the common lodging-houses of London are not always the mysteries of Poverty and Crime.

CHAPTER V
THE WAYS OF CRIME

How big house robberies are planned—The up-to-date burglar—The fine art of crime—The brutal assaults that are paid for—How a man is marked—An assault that became murder.

THE crimes of London are the crimes of humanity plus those of a great city. There are amateur criminals and professional criminals. The amateur criminal is the man or woman who yields to a sudden impulse or the stress of circumstance. The professional criminal is the man or woman who makes a business of crime, and practises it for the purpose of profit.

Education and modern invention have brought our methods of crime to a fine art, and there are criminal organizations which, having brains and capital behind them, are able to realize immense sums annually for division among the partners.

The mystery of many a jewel-robbery which startles the public and baffles the police would be solved if what has long been suspected could only be proved—namely, the existence in London of a system of planting confederates—male and female—in the houses of the wealthy as domestic servants.

The servant so planted is always well-behaved, and inspires the greatest confidence. He or she comes with a personal character that is irreproachable. Let us take an example of the methods resorted to to "place" a confederate.

"A lady going abroad wishes to find a situation for her footman, whom she can thoroughly recommend. Address in the first instance by letter," etc.

The desire to secure a footman who can be thoroughly recommended induces a number of ladies to write.

From the applications sent in, the best addresses are selected, rapid inquiries are made of tradespeople and others, and the lady whose house it is believed will best suit the purpose of the thieves is communicated with.

The footman, who is in league with a band of expert jewel-thieves, is a trained servant. It is necessary that he should be so to retain the place long enough for the plans of the gang to be matured.

He soon finds out the ways of his employers and the whereabouts of the "stuff" that is desired. The rest is easy. He communicates all the necessary information to his colleagues, gives them notice of the arrival of a favourable opportunity, leaves everything arranged to facilitate a noiseless entry into the premises, and has nothing further to do with the "job." These jewel robberies generally take place in the evening, while the family are at dinner at home, or dining out, or at the theatre. No one has any suspicion of the footman. He always arranges to be with the other servants as much as possible at the time the robbery is being skilfully effected.

The lady's maid is a favourite "plant" servant, and is sometimes more useful to the gang than the footman. The lady's maid has frequently possession of her mistress's keys, and she is able to take a "squeeze" of any key that may be required by the burglars, who want to go to work noiselessly and expeditiously.

The "squeeze" is taken by pressing the key in a piece of specially prepared wax. With this impression in his possession, the intending thief can have a similar key made at once. He sometimes comes at the favourable hour armed, not only with a key of the safe or cabinet in which the jewel-case is kept, but with the key of the front door as well. He lets himself in quietly while the family are out, and the servants are downstairs, goes straight to the room in which the jewellery is, unlocks the safe or cabinet, and is out of the house with the plunder in a few minutes.

By obtaining a "squeeze" of a key in an office in which a number of clerks were actually sitting at the time, a safe was once opened while in transit on the South-Eastern Railway, which contained bullion to the value of many thousands of pounds, and the whole of it was successfully carried away.

Some of the biggest jewel-robberies that take place in London are planned, not as they used to be, in low dens and thieves' kitchens or taverns of evil reputation, but in luxuriously furnished houses and elegant flats. When you have made a five or ten thousand pound haul, it is much safer to drive home to a good address with the plunder in your smartly appointed brougham than go off with it in a four-wheel cab to a shabby neighbourhood across the water. The tools necessary for the job can also be carried with more safety in a brougham, and if you have an elegantly attired lady beside you dressed in ball costume, and blazing with jewellery, no policeman is likely to stop your carriage at 4 a.m. to inquire if you have been breaking into a jeweller's shop or a diamond merchant's office.

The expert bank-robber of to-day opens an account at the bank he intends to victimize. Sometimes he has been a customer of the establishment for months before he risks the trick by which the clerk of another bank doing business at the counter is robbed of thousands of pounds' worth of notes. The expert does not do the stealing himself; he merely engages the clerk behind the counter in conversation, and covers the operations of a confederate. This confederate is occasionally attired in the correct costume of a bank-messenger.

The profession of crime to-day has in its ranks men whose manners are those of the diplomatist, whose get-up is faultless, and whose fertility of resource would enable them to make a good living by honest means. But they have become captains of crime, and they prey upon society with a keen enjoyment of the sport.

Some of them carry on their operations upon the strictest business principles. They have their agents in the big cities of the Continent, they speak several languages, and travel about the world. They belong to an international society of malefactors which has frequently in hand at the same time a big job in London, another in Paris, a third in New York, and a fourth in Vienna. They travel first class, put up at the best hotels, and are delightful companions if you get acquainted with them in the railway train or on board ship. Occasionally they combine skill at cards with their other accomplishments, and during the American touring season they travel to and fro on the big liners and make a very fine thing of it.

One of the most dangerous of the fraternity—a man with a world-wide reputation for villainy—was at one time a near neighbour of mine in Regent's Park. He made such a sensation eventually in London that it was thought that a period of retirement would be beneficial to his health and to the welfare of the community. He is now resting, but if he would in his leisure write a truthful account of his adventures in America, London, Australia, Monte Carlo, and Paris, it would be the most thrilling romance of crime that has ever been given to the world.

In a recent celebrated case the Judge described a woman as a Princess of Evil, and said that she had hypnotized wealthy men, and so inspired them with confidence in her.

There are women who have hypnotized men of wealth and position so successfully that they have married half a dozen at short intervals, and acquired possession by that means, not only of family jewels and large sums of money, but of family papers and family secrets, and have found a means of compelling the tricked "husband" to hold his peace, even after the character of the "wife" was discovered.

One woman, not particularly good-looking or in any way captivating, married four wealthy men within two years, quitting each bridegroom "at the church door"—as the melodramas have it; and she drew large sums of money from all of them. This "Princess of Evil" married two of the husbands in London, one in France, and one in America. When one of the London husbands, having discovered that he was a free man, married again, she threatened him with a charge of bigamy unless he paid her a large sum of money.

She might have had the audacity to keep her threats had not her victim had the good sense to write and inform her that if she made any further attempt to annoy him, he would instantly place the matter in the hands of the police, and put up with the unpleasant publicity.

The body of a finely built man was found floating a year or two ago in the Thames with a rope round the neck. A lady, some time after the description of the man had been given in the papers, and the body had been buried as unidentified, came forward and revealed the fact that the man was her husband. She urged that he had been murdered by the friends of another woman whom he had recently married. The two women had met and condoled with each other. The second wife brought an action for nullity, but the first stated by her counsel in open court that she would give no evidence, as her husband had always been good to her. It was after the trial that the man disappeared, and was never seen again until he was taken lifeless from the river, where it was conjectured he had been lying for some weeks.

How the man got into the Thames with a rope round his neck was never discovered. It remains a mystery to this day.

It is not likely that the relatives of the second wife had anything to do with the crime, for they were people in a good social position, and came into open court with the story of the wrong done their kinswoman.

But if a rich person *did* want vengeance wreaked upon an enemy, there are ways and means of bringing it about without any active part being taken by the aggrieved parties.

There are men ready and willing to do anything for a consideration, and more than one brutal assault, which has ended in the death of the victim, and been put down to "hooligans," has been a crime planned and paid for by people of means.

The commissioned crime is a feature of modern London, and it is rarely that the mystery surrounding it is solved.

Let us look in for a moment at a well-known West End bar, much frequented by young men about town, racing men, and certain members of the prize-ring who are well in with the people who make a business of sport. Some of the habitués are gossiping and drinking at the bar or sitting at the little tables. Among them are men of good position in the sporting world, but there are also card-sharpers and tricksters. One or two are pugilists who go to race-meetings to look after or "mind" bookmakers who carry large sums of ready money about with them. Some of these men are respectable and doing well, and would not mix themselves up with a criminal "job." But there are others who are not too particular, provided there is a good chance of doing a "crooked" thing profitably and safely.

One of these men, who is so well in with a certain class of thieves that he can always get back for a consideration a valuable article of jewellery that has been stolen, is standing at the bar drinking, and apparently taking no notice of anyone. But as a matter of fact he is keeping his eye on a young "swell" who is sitting at a little table, talking loudly and boastingly to a man in evening dress who belongs to the cleverest gang of card-sharpers in London.

The young "swell" has come into possession of a fortune, and is seeing life. He is plunging on the turf, and playing cards for large stakes. The sharp is going to ask him to his flat—quite a first-class flat in the West End—and he is going to be "rooked" of a large sum of money.

The man leaning against the bar is studying this young fellow. He has only been put on the job that night, and has been told to come to this bar and make himself thoroughly acquainted with the features of the quarry.

The man who has got a "flat" wants to keep his "find."

He doesn't want him to fall into the hands of a rival gang. So he has put a spy on to watch, and inform him if any overtures are made to the "pigeon" by any other members of the "flash mob."

The spy has studied his man carefully, and will know him again anywhere. So he finishes his drink and leaves the bar. He is instantly followed by a well-dressed man of about forty.

Out in the street the well-dressed man comes abreast of the spy, and says, "Jack, I've got a job for you." Details follow, and the spy is commissioned to find two or three men who will brutally assault a person named at the first convenient opportunity. A plan is agreed upon, and terms arranged. So much for the go-between, so much down to the men engaged, and a large sum to divide among them when the assault has been brought off. Particulars of the person who is to be assaulted, details of his habits, and the place and time at which he is most likely to be caught alone, are given, and the conspirators separate.

Let us now look in at a dirty, ill-lighted beer-house in a gloomy street in one of the most criminal areas of London.

Half a dozen roughs are drinking and smoking in the tap-room. To them enters the man I have called the spy. He asks two of them to come outside with him, and he offers them the job. He satisfies them that the money is right, and guarantees it, for in these cases the principal is never seen. The men engaged know they can accept the guarantee, because if they were bested, the life of the guarantor wouldn't be worth an hour's purchase.

A week later a gentleman returning from town by the last train alights at a Thames-side station. He sets out to walk to his residence. His way lies along a quiet, deserted road.

Someone passing along that road in the small hours finds a man lying insensible on the footpath. He has evidently been brutally knocked about, robbed, and left for dead.

Help is secured, and a doctor endeavours to restore consciousness, but the victim dies without uttering a word.

The deed is put down to footpads, who probably met the gentleman and assaulted him in order to rob him. Every effort is made to trace the guilty men, but without success. The few people who have noticed a trap being driven along the road to London would not connect it with the hired ruffians who committed this midnight crime.

But this assault, which resulted in murder, was commissioned and paid for by a man of means who had a grudge against the victim. This man reads the account of the murder, and is perhaps a little alarmed. He didn't wish it to go as far as that. But he is quite safe. None of the men who assisted in the crime, either passively or actively, are likely to come forward and make any revelations. They have their own necks to think of.

The crime of "bashing"—that is the professional name for it—is far commoner than the peaceful citizens of London imagine. To commit a brutal assault for hire is a means of livelihood practised by certain gangs of ruffians who have their regular haunts and houses of call, where they "attend" to get the "office" of any job that may be going.

A large number of the crimes attributed to hooligans are deliberate plots of this kind. Money is not always the consideration. Sometimes it is good comradeship. A respectable elderly shopkeeper was waylaid and stabbed to death in the Borough a year or two ago. The police could find no motive for the crime, but the mystery was solved eventually by the confession of a young man undergoing five years penal servitude.

The victim had made complaints to the police of a woman, a neighbour, which caused her to be summoned and fined.

The son of the woman was the leader of a gang of young roughs who infested the Borough. He called his band together, and sentence of death was passed upon the "informer." It was many weeks before the old man was out late enough to give the band a chance of executing their captain's orders. But directly the chance came they committed the murder entrusted to them.

In a busy little street leading to a broad West End thoroughfare there is a shop in which a legitimate business is carried on. There is a back shop, divided by a partition from the front, to which special customers go to select from the stock that is kept there; and beyond is an inner office.

The proprietor of the establishment is the head of one of the biggest criminal organizations in London. In that little back shop and that inner office some of the most skilful forgeries of modern times have been arranged. Each member of the gang is a specialist. One, a good-looking young fellow, gets to know servant-maids, and learns from them particulars of their masters' habits. Another frequents billiard-rooms, and gets in with City clerks. Another opens an account at the bank on which the forged cheque is to be drawn, and receives a cheque-book. Then the skilled hands are set to work. One man will fill in the cheque for a large amount, another will forge the signature to it, and the third will drive up in a hurry just as the bank is closing and present it.

The money secured, the man who cashed the cheque passes the proceeds to a confederate who is waiting for him, and takes a train out of London at once. He will receive his share of the plunder by post, and remain at a discreet distance until the hue and cry is over. The gentleman who opened the account and got a cheque-book and drew his balance down to nothing the day before the *coup* was brought off, will probably go away too. But the man who plans and finances burglaries, forgeries, confidence tricks, and swindles on wholesale lines, will remain in town and carry on the business of his highly respectable shop without feeling a moment's anxiety.

The police may have their own ideas about him, but he is much too clever to let them get a scrap of evidence that would connect him with the exploits of the gang of which he is the life and soul.

The wholesale distribution of forged bank-notes which ended in the sensational suicide at the Old Bailey of the principal in the business, was arranged and worked from a room above a little shop in one of the busiest streets of a crowded area. The men who were distributing thousands of forged bank-notes about the country came here for their "parcels" in broad daylight, and passed out with them under the very eyes of the police. On one occasion there were so many people blocking the pavement to look at things exhibited in the shop window that a police-constable had to clear a path for a man with a pocket full of forged bank-notes to pass away with them.

The gang might have continued to circulate the notes with impunity, but for the treachery of a comrade, who betrayed them.

The chief of the gang, though in custody, determined to be revenged upon the informer. He managed to communicate with a woman. She made a beefsteak pie, and in this pie concealed a loaded revolver. The revolver was wrapped up in greaseproof paper.

The pie was delivered to the prisoner when he was being tried at the Old Bailey. He took the revolver into court with him, intending to shoot the informer. But the chance he hoped for was denied him, so when he was sentenced to a long term of penal servitude, the convict put the revolver to his own head and shot himself dead.

How a prisoner kept in close custody could obtain a loaded revolver and carry it with him into the dock was for a long time an unsolved mystery.

I learnt the truth standing in the room where the pie was made. It is this fertility of resource which enables the modern criminal to outwit the modern detective, and makes mysterious the ways of crime.

CHAPTER VI
IN THE CITY OF REFUGE

Escaped from the land of the Tsar—What they learn—Robbed at the frontier—How they reached London—The terrors of rejection—How some outcasts get on.

IT is six o'clock on Sunday evening. It has been a wild, wet, February day, but with the twilight the rain has ceased, and a mist has come up from the river, wrapping the East End in a cold grey gloom.

Outside the newspaper shops in Aldgate flaring placards announce the latest disaster to the Russian army at the seat of war, and the internal troubles with which the empire of the Tsar is faced.

Looking at the placards, the war seems far away. The unfamiliar—to our eyes and ears almost barbarous—names of the Manchurian towns and rivers suggest illimitable space between the East in which we find ourself and the Far East where a yellow and a white race are writing history with swords for pens and seas of blood for ink, and are punctuating the pages with shot and shell.

Yet only a stone's-throw from where we stand in High Street, Aldgate, we may study real flesh and blood pages torn from the story of the war between Russia and Japan.

Thousands of Londoners pass daily along the great East End highway, and have not the faintest shadow of suspicion that within a few yards of them are hundreds of soldiers—men who have fought in the present war—men who have been in Japanese hospitals—men who have fled to escape further service, who have endured the most terrible hardships, who have, some of them, seen their comrades shot down by their side—Russian soldiers killed by Russian soldiers.

If we turn off the main road and strike down Leman Street, we shall come to a large private house, on the door-plate of which the words "The Jews' Free Shelter" are inscribed.

A few strange-looking men in sea-stained coats and high boots are standing about on the pavement, silent and solemn, with a dull, anxious look in their eyes.

We recognize the Jewish Shelter, look at the little groups, say to ourselves, "More alien immigrants," and perhaps pass on.

But if we go round to the back of the house we find ourselves in a narrow street which ends in a dead wall. And in this street, standing four deep in a line that stretches right away to the wall itself, are hundreds of the soldiers of the Tsar. They are all Jews, they have all escaped from Russia at the risk of their lives. Most of them had only a few roubles in their pockets. But they have come from Russia—some even from Manchuria—and they are here to-night in the quiet, deserted London street waiting their turn to go before the committee which is sitting in the big room of the Shelter to hear their stories, and see what can be done to help them to make a new home thousands of miles away across the seas.

Two London policemen and an inspector are standing in the roadway. They are there to preserve order among these six or seven hundred Russian reservists. But their office is a sinecure. These hunted men, fresh from a land of tyranny, are silent, cowed, incapable of anything but the blindest obedience to the authority of the land to which they have fled seeking a City of Refuge.

There is no need for the policemen to speak to them. If they did, no one in the thickly packed mob of men would understand them. None of the refugees speak a word of English; Yiddish—the German-Jewish jargon—is their mother tongue; but most of them, having been in the army, speak a little Russian.

The inspector, finding that the crowd is spreading over into the roadway, makes a motion with his hand, and the men press closer together. They understand the gesture, and obey it as quickly as they would obey the upraised whip of the Cossack.

They have not yet learnt that in England no one in authority will knock them about or kick them. If they were so used they would not show any resentment. It is the way in which they have been habitually treated in Russia. Sometimes one of their own number, placed in temporary authority to assist the staff of the Shelter, clears a way for someone to pass by, thrusting his compatriots back with a little violence. He does not understand that there is anything unusual in this method of giving an order. When it is explained to him that in England we don't lay hands upon peaceable people in this way, he is astonished. What a wonderful country! The great people don't knock a poor Jew off the footpath! They speak to him civilly! It takes a newly arrived Russian Jew many days to understand that he is going to be treated like a human being, and that even the police will not kick him or hit him on the head if he is unfortunate enough to be in the way.

This Sunday evening there are more than six hundred refugees waiting to enter the doors of the Shelter and go before the committee. During the week over a thousand have arrived. They are mostly the reservists who have been called up and have fled to avoid further service. They have served once— many of them have only just finished their time and returned to their wives and families. They don't want to go to Manchuria. They are Jews; and the

Jew serves the Tsar under grievous disabilities. He cannot rise in rank. If he is killed, no information is forwarded to his relatives. In Russia, a Jew is outside the pale of humanity.

Let us pass into the building. We have left a packed army of men standing dumb and motionless outside. Here in a kind of courtyard is another silent and motionless crowd. Two hundred men at least are crowded together, and not a sound comes from their lips. They look like statues of despair. Their one feeling is of relief that they are now inside the Shelter, and so their chance of getting before the committee to-night is better.

We pass from this courtyard to an inner room. It is packed. We have seen already nearly a thousand deserters from the Tsar's army. The Shelter cannot provide accommodation for a tenth of this vast army of fugitives. But every one will get a ticket that will give him food and a lodging. So much these unhappy immigrants know. What they do not know is whether they will be helped to America, to Canada, to the Argentine, to any of the lands where there are Jewish colonies, and where they will be able to toil and save, and in time send for the wives and children left behind in Russia to join them.

All of them have paid the fare to London. Some of them have hidden about them the fare to America or Canada. But others are penniless. They have been robbed at the Russian frontier. They have had to part with every rouble to pass the officials. Sometimes they have given up everything to the sentries to save themselves from being shot down.

It is a peaceful Sunday evening in London, but here are all the horrors of war. And of all London's myriad people, only a few active sympathizers in the Jewish community know of this human tragedy working itself out in London's heart.

Let us leave these unhappy ones massed together in quiet street, in crowded yard, and in the packed room, and pass into another room in which the committee are now sitting, as they will sit on far into the night, examining every man in turn as to his trade, his means, and his prospect of earning a living if room is found for him in one of the ships which the sympathy and philanthropy of their co-religionists have secured for these poor wandering Jews.

Let us sit at one of the long deal tables at which members of the committee are cross-examining the applicants for guidance and assistance, receiving money, making out tickets, and dispatching the refugees to various parts of the world.

A squarely built man of about thirty, pale, haggard, and with a hunted look in his eyes, comes forward. He tells his story. He is a builder of wooden houses. He had served his time, and had been home but for a few weeks, when he was ordered to rejoin. He talked the matter over with some fellow-reservists. They made up their minds to escape. They sold their possessions, got together a little money from their friends, and started. There were six of them, and they got into a train. After travelling a long time they came to a station, at which the carriage was entered by soldiers, who dragged four of the company out. The men were charged with being deserters. Two of the company remained in the train; the man standing now at the table was one of them. But they knew their turn would come, so they scrambled out on the other side of the line and ran for their lives across the country.

A party of soldiers started in pursuit. The men reached a river and leapt in. The soldiers fired and killed one. The man at the table swam to the opposite bank and made good his escape. For many hours he went on and on in his wet clothes, shivering with cold, his limbs benumbed. He endured the most terrible privations; but at last he reached the frontier, got into Germany, and with the money concealed about him purchased a ticket to London.

He stands before us in London to-night, waiting to know where the committee can send him for the roubles which he still has left. He receives a ticket for a ship leaving for Canada, drops a knee in the Russian manner of salutation, and goes forth gleefully into the street to think out the future in the London lamplight.

The man who takes his place is a fine-looking young fellow. Where has he come from? When he is asked, he answers, "Mukden."

Everyone at the table looks up at that. Is it possible that a Russian deserter has made his way from Mukden to Whitechapel? Yes. Here are the facts vouched for, proved beyond dispute.

This man had been serving a year in the Mukden garrison. During a sortie he, with some hundreds of other Russian soldiers, was forced on to a frozen river. The ice gave way, and they all fell in, the Japs firing at them from the bank. An officer in the same regiment as the Jewish soldier was wounded in the head, and was sinking, when the Jew got hold of him and swam with him to the bank. The officer was taken to the hospital, and the Jewish soldier followed him there shortly afterwards, suffering from pneumonia.

The Jew got well, but the officer died after lingering some weeks. Before his death he got the Jew called to him, and said, "You've been good to me—here, take these three hundred roubles—all I have—and get out of this hell as soon as you."

The Jew managed to escape, got rid of his uniform, and made his way across Siberia, now tramping, now travelling by chance conveyances. He reached Moscow in ten weeks. Thence he came to the Shelter in Whitechapel.

Here is a well-set-up young fellow; he is six feet, a height not common among Russian Jews. He wants to go to America, where he has friends. This is the story he tells. Again it shows the Russian officer in a new light. I will call the man Marcovitch. Even in these pages it would not be wise to give his real name, for the agents of the Tsar have keen eyes and are everywhere.

He was orderly to the colonel of the regiment. When the regiment was about to leave on active service, the colonel thought that Marcovitch was too good to go out and get shot. He did not, however, like to tell him in so many words to desert, so this is what he did. The regiment was stationed on the German frontier, so the colonel told Marcovitch he wanted him to cross over into the nearest German town to make some purchases for him there. At the same time he gave him two sealed envelopes, which Marcovitch was not to open till he got into German territory. When he opened them he found that one contained instructions how to get to England, and the other rouble notes for £10. Marcovitch took the hint and the money, and arrived safely in Whitechapel.

These are exceptional cases. Most of the stories that are told are tales of misery and despair, of homes broken up, of wives and children left behind, of terrible journeys and hairbreadth escapes, of freedom purchased at a price almost as terrible as death itself.

Almost every man of the hundreds thronging the Shelter and its annexes tonight has served his time with the colours. Hardly any are recruits. Most of the men have left dear ones behind them—dear ones who are still ignorant of the fate that may have befallen the fugitive. And all of them are prepared to go anywhere—to the most distant parts of the earth—if only they can be free to work and make a new home for their kindred in some land of liberty.

All, before they are sent away, even though they have the money to pay their passage, will have to pass a medical examination. If they are suffering from certain forms of disease they will be refused on the other side. The victims of persecution in Russia and Roumania have ere this made the journey of thousands of miles to the New World only to be refused admittance, and to be sent back again across the sea. It is a terrible picture to dwell upon—a miserable fellow-creature, ill, weak, despairing, refused a foothold everywhere—a storm-tossed human waif, whose one crime is that he dared to cling to the faith of his fathers in the land of the Great White Tsar.

Those who cannot hope to be received in America or Canada, or who are unfit to be sent to the Jewish colonies, are told so plainly, and at once. Every effort is made to get them out of London, and they are kindly treated.

But these Jewish immigrants are never utterly disheartened. Self-preservation is an instinct of the race.

I saw a man turned away regretfully by the committee one night. He had but a few shillings in his pocket. A week later I saw the same man with a basket in the Lane selling stockings at a shilling a pair. A fortnight later he had a little barrow with goods for sale on it. When I heard from him last, he had sent to Russia for his wife, and had opened a little shop in the Ghetto.

There are men in the city of London engaged in large businesses, and employing hundreds of Christian hands in manufactures not previously carried on in England, and these men came from Russia and Poland poor persecuted Jews, with but a few shillings in the world to call their own. If I were to make a list of the big Jewish manufacturers and tradesmen, and Jewish men of learning and of science, who came to this country poor alien immigrants, the revelation would be an astounding one.

But we must not stay now to look back or to look forward. The people to whose stories we are listening to-day have left the past behind them, and their future is an unknown quantity. The present is to them a problem which shuts out all other considerations.

Here is a refugee who fled from a city of massacre. He had been wounded in a riot at Ekaterinoslav. During the riot his brother disappeared, and it was supposed that he had been killed and quietly buried by the authorities.

When this man gives his name it is a peculiar one. A member of the committee remembers that some time previously a man with a similar name had come to the Shelter from Russia, and had been sent to America. The books are referred to, and a full description of the man is found.

It is the brother who was supposed to be dead. The poor applicant is overjoyed. He receives his ticket for America, and goes from the room almost hysterical with joy. He is going across the seas to find in the new land the brother whom he had mourned as dead.

A young woman comes before the committee with tears in her eyes. She has her ticket for the Argentine. What does she want?

She tells a pathetic little story. Five years ago her only sister left Russia and came to London. She sent her address to her relatives. The girl who is now before the committee has accompanied her husband, a reservist. When she left home she took her sister's last letter with the address on it and put it with her few belongings. She has lost the letter. She has been all day tramping about trying to find anyone who can tell her where her sister is living. To-morrow she will have to leave London for the Argentine. She may be quite close to her sister at this very moment—the sister she loves—but she must go away to-morrow, and in all human probability they will never meet again.

What can be done? Nothing. To find a certain woman in London, who left Russia five years ago, is beyond the power of the committee. They can only offer the weeping girl their sympathy.

Here is a boy of fourteen—a sturdy little fellow. He steps up boldly to the table. Where are his parents? He has none. His father and mother were killed in the massacre of Kischineff. He has obtained enough money of friends and sympathizers in Kischineff to make his way to England. He has come alone from Kischineff to London, and he asks the committee to help him. The boy's story is a pitiful one. The committee investigate his case, and it is decided to send the lonely little voyager to the Jewish Orphanage at Jerusalem.

The quiet of the Christian Sabbath night has settled on London as we make our way from the Jewish Shelter to the wide thoroughfare that leads to the deserted and silent streets of the City.

But outside the Shelter in that grey back street a serried mass of silent suffering still waits dumbly, patiently, for the dawn of a new life.

Far away in the Pales of Settlement women and children are wondering and weeping—wondering if the husband, the father, is alive or dead, if he has reached the City of Refuge or been captured as he fled—if he has died by the way, or been shot down by the soldiers of the Tsar.

They will hear in time. Letters and cards are on the way to them bearing the London post-mark and the unfamiliar stamp with the head of King Edward VII of England upon it.

CHAPTER VII
BEHIND THE SCENES

The tragedy of the smiling face—Starving at their work—From manager to super—A fallen star—A terrible life drama—The brighter side of the profession.

Fortune has smiled upon the happy favourites of the footlights. Never was the glamour of the stage more powerful than it is to-day; never were young men and young women more eager to revel in the limelight and leave the dull duties of everyday life for the gay Bohemianism of the boards.

The world, that judges only by what it sees, looks upon the life of the fortunate few as typical of the theatrical life generally. Of the hidden mysteries of the player-folk's pilgrimage it knows nothing. It hears of the magnificent salaries of the stars, it sees the portraits of pretty actresses week after week in the illustrated papers, it is led to believe that every girl who joins the chorus of certain theatres has the chance of marrying a millionaire, and it understands that the members of touring companies go gaily about the world on a picnic arrangement and have all their expenses paid.

It is not upon the parade-ground that one learns what the life of a soldier means; it is upon the battlefield. We see our actors and our actresses and the merry entertainers of the variety halls and palaces on the parade-ground. Very few of us see them upon the battlefield, in the time of storm and stress, when the issue of the struggle is one of life and death.

The hidden mysteries of the stage it is not permitted to the outside world to penetrate.

Kings and queens in historical romance, princes and princesses in pantomime, duchesses in society comedy, of my working life in close communion with the warm-hearted children of Thespis, lift a corner of the veil, it will be but to show how much there is to admire in the men and women who, out of the rays of the limelight, often lead brave, self-sacrificing, and very human lives.

Let us sit for a while in the waiting-room of a well-known London agent, and listen to the boys and girls who come there day after day in the hope of getting an engagement.

There are no anxious faces. The young actor does not wear his heart upon his sleeve. The young actress does not let her professional sisters see that she is breaking down under the strain of hope deferred.

The conversation is light, almost frivolous. It is a merry world for everybody in theatre land, and even when four o'clock comes, and the hope of the day is over, the boys and girls will go chattering out into the street and bid each other a smiling good-day.

But there is a change in many of the faces when the Strand is left behind. There are tears in the eyes of the girl who was smiling so brightly a few minutes ago. The man who stepped with such a jaunty air along Garrick Street drops his chin, and his face grows stern.

There are people at home—a mother and a sister, perhaps—dependent upon the actress, and she has been out of an engagement for a couple of months. But the girl must keep up appearances. She must be neatly dressed and look happy. To acknowledge defeat, to dress poorly, would "let her down" and injure her prospects.

The young actor may be married. He has a wife and child at home. The summer has gone—how he got through it he hardly knows himself. Now the autumn has come, and he is still out of an engagement. If he could sing, he would do what many another young actor does. He would join a troupe of pierrots—of seaside minstrels. He would sing on the beach, in the streets, anywhere, to keep the wolf from the door. But he is only an earnest and capable young actor, and he can't get an engagement.

These unlucky ones are young, and hope will buoy them up for a time. They will weather the storm, and presently they will be rehearsing, and the stress will be lighter.

But even when the engagement is secured and the rehearsals begin, there is a terrible time to get through.

Many pieces are rehearsed for six or seven weeks, and during that time there may be no salary. However distant from the theatre the actor and actress live, they may have to walk—'buses cost money.

I have known an actor and his wife, who were compelled to ride because the distance was too great to walk, go for days with only two pennyworth of food each in order to pay the train fare. But they were both capable and conscientious artists, and had always had excellent notices. A series of short runs had exhausted their resources. This is what had happened to them in one year. An engagement and a month's rehearsal. The play ran a fortnight. They were out for three weeks. An engagement and six weeks' rehearsal. The play ran a month, then they were two months out. Then an engagement in the provinces. The tour, owing to bad business, terminated earlier than was expected. Then out at Whitsuntide and out all the summer. At the end of August came an engagement to open at the end of September, and a month's rehearsal before a farthing of salary was touched.

But if you meet these unfortunate Thespians they will be bright and cheery, and never let you see a sign of the care that is gnawing at their heart-strings.

Years ago I met a brother dramatist on the morning that the news reached England of the suicide under terrible circumstances of an actor whose name was well known in the West for many years. I said that I feared things had been going badly with the poor fellow for some time. Then my friend told me of a pathetic incident.

A year previously the actor came to lunch with him one Sunday by invitation. A joint of roast beef was the principal item, and the guest excused himself for having a second helping. He had had a long walk, and it had given him an appetite.

The host turned his head a little to look out of the window at something that was passing. But there was a mirror that reflected the guest. In the mirror the host saw the poor fellow slip a slice of beef from his plate into the folds of a handkerchief he had in his hand. He was taking the meat home to his wife.

In the days of their vogue the couple had drawn a joint salary of £50 a week. But something happened. Their vogue passed, and for three years they did nothing, sinking gradually into something akin to absolute want, but hiding it from all the world.

"Fifty pounds a week, and come to that!" the prudent may exclaim. But there are plenty of expenses to eat up salaries at the best of times, and the thrift must be great that can enable comparatively young professionals to stand the strain of no income for three years.

If these are the vicissitudes of an actor's life while youth and strength are assets, it is not difficult to imagine how terrible must be the struggle for existence when age comes to those who have been unable to provide for it.

It is then that the problem faces most workers, but there is not in ordinary callings the sharp contrast that exists among the unfortunate of the theatre world.

To have money, friends, fame, and public favour at one period of your life, and then to know poverty, loneliness, neglect—that is the experience that adds bitterness to the cup of sorrow many an old favourite has to drain to the dregs before the merciful curtain falls.

It happened to me once, behind the scenes, to find lying on the mimic battlefield of a Drury Lane drama three corpses, and each of the "supers" who impersonated a soldier, with nothing to say and nothing to do but fall down at a given cue, had been a popular actor, and the lessee and manager of a London theatre. On the stage of the great national theatre I saw in a pantomime procession of Shakespearean characters King Lear represented by an actor who had once played the part on those very boards as the bright particular star of the evening.

The theatrical profession is the most generous in the world. When it hears of a sad case, the more fortunate comrades of one who has fallen by the way come to the rescue. A private subscription is made; a benefit is organized; the sympathy shown is whole-hearted, generous, and practical. But it often happens that the tragedy is only discovered by accident. The wounded comrade has hidden himself away and suffered in silence, too proud to let his pitiable condition be known.

In my wanderings along the shores on which our social wreckage is cast, I come frequently upon men and women who have strutted their hour upon the stage—men and women who had at one time fortune at their feet in the entertainment world, and have come to the workhouse or the common lodging-house.

To the people with whom they associate they are unknown. When they have their day out from the workhouse, when they come ragged and wretched from the lodging-house, and pass the hours as best they can, they attract no attention.

A woman in weather-stained clothes, with a battered hat on her unkempt hair, with the skirts of her dress caked with the mud of the streets, does not appeal to the curiosity of the well-to-do people who pass her by. They do not imagine that there is any mystery about this woman, still young, still good-looking, who has sunk so low. They let her go by, and if they think about her at all, it is as a tramp—a homeless vagabond who sleeps in the parks or on the Embankment.

But if they had known when she had passed them who this woman was, everyone would have turned to look after her. For her portrait was for years in the illustrated papers, the dramatic critics wrote of her enthusiastically, and the leading managers competed for her services.

She was found one evening in the park, ill, dazed, apparently dying. She had crawled under a hedge to sleep, and there she had attracted the attention of some tramps who were "camping" near at hand. One of them went and found a policeman, and the poor woman was carried to the workhouse infirmary. There, by certain old letters found upon her, her identity was revealed, and presently it became known to the profession that one whom they had all regarded with affection and esteem was homeless, penniless, starving.

The response to an appeal was generous; everything that sympathy and help and skilful treatment could do was done; but the once famous actress only recovered a little of her strength to pass away soon afterwards in an asylum.

The life dramas in which the dwellers in limelight-land play a part are often stranger, more romantic, more pathetic, than any written play in which they simulate the human emotions for the entertainment of the public.

The causes of catastrophe are many, and are often obscure. There came to me a year or two ago two sisters. They were young actresses, and wanted parts in a forthcoming play with which I wat associated. They stayed for a few minutes after I had told them that all the parts were filled; they patted my little dog, and asked to see a little white cat of which I had occasionally written in the "Referee."

They bade me a smiling good-bye, and went out, apparently in the best of spirits. A few days afterwards they were found lying dead side by side in their lodgings. They had agreed to die together, and had taken poison. Young and beautiful, with the world all before them, they had broken down almost at the outset of their career under the strain of professional disappointment.

In the days of my youth I knew intimately a famous manager in the entertainment world. He was originally a waiter in a well-known restaurant, but he had ability and pluck, and he became in time the proprietor of a famous variety palace, and some equally famous pleasure gardens. He was also a caterer and contractor on a large scale.

In the days of his prosperity he drove a six-hundred-guinea pair of horses in his phaeton, and the brougham in which he was whirled about in the evening was as well known to the public as that in which Adah Isaacs Menken drove nightly to Astley's when she was drawing all London over Westminster Bridge to see her in "Mazeppa."

Many years afterwards, when the brilliant star of the variety firmament had disappeared, and no one knew what had become of him, I was on a penny steamer on the Thames. A poor old fellow with a greasy cap on his head was waiting about and taking orders for any refreshments the passengers might require. He passed me once and looked at me earnestly. Presently he brought a bottle of beer to two men sitting by me, and then I recognized him. The man, whose name had been one to conjure with in connection with variety enterprise, was the steward of a penny steamer on the Thames.

But when we look behind the scenes of theatrical life it is not always the note of tragedy that greets us. There is a fairer and a sunnier side.

Ten years ago a young girl determined to be an actress—had made her way to London—the city of her dreams. It had been a rough journey. In the provinces she had joined a small opera company. When there was any money taken the manager obligingly gave some of it on account of salaries to the artists. When times were bad they had to go without. So it came that the finding of lodgings was a terrible task. When you have no money—and you can't take your luggage into apartments, for fear it should be kept for the rent—very few doors are open to you. In one country town the little girl, failing to get a room, went and sat in a shed in a field and cried herself to sleep there. She woke up at one in the morning with a thunder and lightning storm raging. She ran out into the roadway, and a kind policeman took her to his wife, who gave her a bed for the night.

One day, the company being near London, she left it, and, having a few shillings in her pocket, took a train which landed her at Liverpool Street. She found lodgings in the Whitechapel Road, and thought that London was a very busy place, but she didn't think the people dressed very grandly.

In the Whitechapel Reading Room she read the "Era," and saw an advertisement for chorus ladies at Earl's Court. She walked from Whitechapel to Earl's Court, and failed to see the manager. Then she walked back again, and, passing Hyde Park, went into it, and, tired and hungry and broken-hearted, sat down on a seat.

It was the fashionable hour of the afternoon, and the Park was crowded with carriages and elegantly dressed people. The young actress, with nothing in her pocket, and terror of the future in her heart, sat and watched the wealth and luxury of London for a little while. In the bitterness of her despair she almost *hated* the people for being so prosperous and so happy. She burst into tears, and, unable to look any longer at a scene which only emphasized her own misery, she rose and walked, weary and footsore, back to the Whitechapel Road.

That was ten years ago. To-day it is again the fashionable hour, and the Park is crowded. In an elegant victoria sits a charming young lady, daintily dressed, smiling and happy. Every now and then she smiles and bows, and returns the salutation of someone who knows her.

This happy young lady in the victoria is the little actress who sat in the Park and cried because she had not even the money for a 'bus to take her back to the Whitechapel lodging from which she had set out in the morning to walk to Earl's Court.

Twelve years ago a girl of eighteen, thin, white-faced, and none too warmly clad for the bitter winter day, came back wearily to her home. Her father, an actor, had been dead six months. When his affairs were settled, it was found that there was nothing for his wife and daughter. What little he had left was not sufficient to pay his creditors. So the widow made a struggle to keep a home for herself and child. Two rooms were furnished, and the girl looked about for work on the stage. She got a small engagement, then her mother fell ill, and the situation became serious. Then she was out of work again, and the rent had been unpaid for six weeks. The landlord would give only a few days' further grace, and then——

The girl went to her mother's room and fell on a chair by the sick woman's bed. "Nothing yet, mother—nothing yet," she wailed. "What will become of us?"

To-day! A stately house in the fairest English county. It stands in magnificent grounds. If you peer through the gates of the park that lies around it you will see the fine old mansion grandly grey against a background of noble trees.

Presently the park gates open and a carriage comes through them. There are a few villagers in the roadway, and as the carriage passes the women curtsey and the men raise their hats.

The young lady in the carriage is the Lady Bountiful of the place. All the tenants love her, and have loved her from the day she left the stage to come as the new mistress of the Hall to live among them. The middle-aged lady sitting by her side is her mother. They are driving to the station to meet the Lady Bountiful's husband. He has been in London to take part in a debate in the House of Lords.

When last we saw the Lady Bountiful and her companion they were in two furnished rooms, and the girl, terrified at the thought of being homeless, was weeping by her mother's bedside, and wailing, "What will become of us?"

CHAPTER VIII
THE HOUSES OF TRAGEDY

The discovery of the box—And what it contained—The mystery of the coat-cellar—A dreary quarter—A house with a past—Another trunk mystery.

THERE are streets and squares and terraces in London which have been renamed in order that they may no longer be associated in the public mind with the dark deeds of which they have been the scene.

Sometimes, where the renaming has been a difficult one, the houses have been renumbered. But many remain as they were, and Londoners pass them daily and hourly, little dreaming of the drama that once made them notorious.

Let us this bright spring morning take a trip round London and look at some of the houses which a few years ago were the scenes of tragedy and mystery.

We are in a quiet square of well-built, neatly-painted residences. There is an air of comfort and well-to-do-ness about them which bespeaks the "genteel" neighbourhood. The windows are gracefully curtained, the knockers and bells are highly polished, the steps are scrupulously clean. The window-boxes are filled with flowers.

Look well at the house with the turquoise-blue window-boxes. A canary is hanging in the dining-room and singing merrily in the morning sunshine. As we watch, the door opens and a nursemaid comes carefully down the steps with a baby in a perambulator. Two prettily-dressed little girls follow. At the open doorway a young mother stands and watches her little ones as they start hill of childish merriment for their morning walk.

It is a pretty scene, and we know that the four walls of the house frame a picture of happy English home-life. But some years ago there lay in the room in which the canary is singing a corded box. At the front door stood a van on which this box was about to be loaded.

There is another little square five minutes' walk away. On the balcony of one of the houses at the far end a charming girl in a pink blouse is standing. She is leaning over the balcony and talking to some girl friends who have come out of a neighbouring house.

Presently a peal of girlish laughter rings out on the soft May air, and the girls wave their hands to each other in token of adieu.

The pretty girl in the pink blouse goes back again into the room, and as we move away there comes through the open window an air from the latest Gaiety success.

Both these houses belonged at one time to an elderly clergyman. One was empty—the one in which the Gaiety music is being played—and a workman was employed in doing it up that it might be re-let.

The old clergyman went out one morning to see how the repairs were going on, and that was the last that was seen of him for some time.

His elderly housekeeper at his residence in the other square expected him back to dinner. But instead of her master the workman came. That was the last that was seen of the old housekeeper for some time.

A few days later a van stood at the door. The caretaker, a workman, explained that he had been left in charge and had to send a box away. The vanman picked up the box to carry it out, and found his hand stained with blood.

He uttered a cry of alarm and exclaimed, "What does this mean?" Then the workman ran out of the house and the van-man ran after him. The fugitive, who had hurriedly swallowed a dose of laudanum, was arrested by a policeman. Other constables proceeded to the house and opened the box.

In it was the body of the housekeeper. She had been strangled with a rope, which was still round her neck. The rope had been drawn so tightly that it had forced blood from the victim's mouth. The murderer had not calculated on this, and owed the detection of his crime to the circumstance.

Search was made at the house in the other square, and the body of the clergyman was found buried in the drain.

That is the story of two houses in quiet Chelsea squares. In the one we have just seen a charming girl chatting with her friends, and we have heard her playing the piano merrily.

The happy young mother who stands at the door of the other house has no knowledge of the tragedy that once darkened her dwelling-place. In the room where the murder was committed her children romp and play.

Here is one of the most aristocratic thoroughfares in London. From the windows of the beautiful houses you can look upon the green glories of Hyde Park and watch the gay scenes of the Ladies' Mile.

Some of the houses are huge mansions, others are bijou residences. The house to which I would direct your attention once came into the latter category, but it has been rebuilt and enlarged, and the old premises have been absorbed in the new. The house was taken for the season some years ago by a young professional lady and her mother. The young lady paid a visit to some friends from Saturday to Monday. On Monday afternoon she returned, and, knocking, was unable to gain admittance. She had taken her maid with her. Her mother had been left for the Sunday with one servant only in the house—the cook, a foreigner.

When eventually admission was obtained, the young lady, in a state of alarm, searched the house for her mother. She found her lying dead in one of the lower rooms. She had been strangled and dragged with a rope round her neck into the pantry. Money and jewels had been taken, and the foreign cook had disappeared.

The murderess was arrested some time afterwards in Paris, was brought to London, tried, found guilty, condemned, and respited.

As we stand and gaze at the house which bears the old number to-day, we see no sign of its tragic history. There is nothing to suggest that one woman who lived in it was murdered and another tried for her life. At the door an electric brougham stands waiting. An elegantly-dressed young lady comes out and enters it. A footman follows her carrying a dainty lap-dog. The little creature is adorned with a light blue bow. The footman places it in the brougham beside its young mistress.

The dainty lap-dog and the elegant young lady are among the occupants of the premises on which not many years ago a woman lay strangled, and from which a murderess fled.

A house in a big square of boarding-houses and hotels. A house now let out for offices and business purposes, but with a portion of it inhabited, and servants on the premises. Scores of people pass it daily and see nothing in it to arrest their attention. The servants and employées of the house go about undisturbed by any thought of the tragedy once enacted within its walls. One of the servants goes every day to the coal-cellar and fills the scuttles from the black mass that lies around.

But in that coal-cellar there lay concealed for months the body of an old lady who suddenly disappeared, who one day wrote to her friends, and from that day forth was never seen again until she was found a strangled corpse with coals and rubbish piled upon her in the corner of the cellar. There were arrests for that murder, but no one was found guilty of it. The crime still remains one of the mysteries of London.

Many years before she came to her end I knew the victim personally. For some months I saw her almost daily. I ceased to visit the health resort where she was one of the best-known habituées, and in time forgot her.

I remembered her again only when her murder revealed the fact that she had been living a lonely lodging-house life for years in London, and had disappeared; to be found in circumstances which added one more mystery of crime to the capital's crowded record.

Not long ago I found myself late at night in a dark, ill-lighted street in the south-east of London. I had been through an area of narrow byways and alleys that has long been the despair of the authorities, an area that to walk through at night requires a certain amount of confidence in one's powers of self-protection. Shadowy figures crept here and there in the darkness, and now and then in the distance were the sounds of conflict.

It was impossible to recognize the features of anyone who passed me. The ramshackle houses that lined the muddy lanes—one cannot call these unpaved byways streets—had in them only a glimmer of light, and many of them were without even that.

These long, narrow lanes of slum dwellings meandered in and out and crossed each other till they became a maze. When in the pitch darkness I found myself faced with a dead wall through which a narrow opening had been cut, and discovered that it was the entrance to another maze of alleys, I turned back and groped my way to the distant lights of a street in which I should at least be able to see what sort of people were round about me.

The street, when I reached it, was gloomy enough, but there were one or two little shops in it. One was a fried-fish shop, which threw a certain amount of light upon the muddy roadway; the other was the shop of a general dealer.

The shop stood at the corner of the lane up which I came, and in the lane was a side entrance, a black wooden door which led to the yard at the back of the house.

Through this door not very long ago a man passed bearing two sacks. Those sacks he put upon a van which he had hired, and drove away with them. He drove to an empty house in the suburbs which he had taken, and that night he dug a deep hole in the garden, put the sacks into it, and covered them up. They contained the bodies of a man, a woman, and a child.

It was close on midnight when I turned the corner, but the shop was still open. There were no customers in it, but through the open door I could see into the back parlour. An old man sat there alone, smoking his pipe and looking into the dying embers of the fire.

The shop had changed hands twice since the murder. Country folks had taken it, ignorant of its history, had found out the terrible tragedy that had been enacted on the premises, and had left again.

I wondered as I looked at the old man if he knew the story of his home.

I have in my possession the letters the murderer wrote from the condemned cell to the mother of his child. They are well written, and convey a suggestion of refined feeling, which is remarkable when one remembers the brutal crime the man committed for a paltry profit. After the murder he remained alone in the house with his victims the long night through, and as soon as he had succeeded in removing the remains he set about to plan another crime of a similar character.

He intended to murder a man whom he had lured to his house, then go to the shop where the intended victim's wife was alone, murder her, and take possession of the business in exactly the same way that he had taken possession of the little shop of his first victim.

Whenever I look late at night into that shop window I am fascinated, for the whole scene reacts itself, and in fancy I see the man—whom I saw tried and condemned—sitting in the little parlour and planning the removal in the morning of the "sacks" through that little black door in the side street.

A small, semi-detached house in a dull, deserted side street of Kentish Town. In the front a little grass plot; in the windows a few pots of ferns. A curtain is drawn aside and a young woman looks up at the sky. She is wondering, probably, if the weather is going to clear up and be fine for her afternoon walk. Two little boys come along and seat themselves on the doorstep. One has a mouth-organ and plays "At the Old Bull and Bush," while his small companion listens critically.

A sleek black cat creeps through the railings, settles down on the little grass plot, and begins to perform an elaborate toilet.

If I were to say that there is nothing in the scene to suggest tragedy, it would not be true. There is, at least, something in the neighbourhood, something in the street, something in the house that suggest mystery. And we are looking upon the scene of a tragedy which was a mystery for a time.

In a room in this house a young woman murdered one afternoon a young mother and her child. Down the steps on which the two boys are seated with the mouth organ the murderess, a few hours later, wheeled a perambulator covered over with a cloth. Beneath the cloth lay the bodies of her victims. The perambulator broke down with the weight near some rough ground on which building operations were in progress. The woman left the bodies— one at the back of a new building, the other some distance away. She wheeled the broken perambulator as far as Hamilton Terrace and went back to the little house and slept there.

All London rang next day with the discovery of the murdered woman; the body of the baby was not found till later on. The body of the woman lay at the mortuary for identification. Two young women came to see it. One, the sister of the victim, recognized it; the woman who accompanied her said that she was mistaken. A police official was present, and something in the second woman's conduct aroused his suspicions.

He ascertained her address, and sent police officers to it to search the house. The condition of one room left no doubt that it had been the scene of a terrible tragedy.

The woman was convicted and hanged. Whatever the motive of the murder was, it did not transpire at the trial. Many people believed it to be an act of insanity, with jealousy as the root of it.

On the night of the crime the husband of the murdered woman called at the house to see the murderess. He had no idea then that a tragedy had happened. He found that the woman was out, and he tore off the top of a "Pall Mall Gazette" he had with him, wrote on it a message in lead pencil, and left it on the kitchen table. "Sorry you are out," was part of the message. It was not until days afterwards that he learnt the woman had gone out that evening instead of waiting in to see him as she had promised that she would do.

All the details of the ghastly tragedy come back to me as I look to-day at the melancholy little house. If the boys with the mouth-organ knew the story of the perambulator that jolted down the steps upon which they sit, they would probably shift their ground and take their *al fresco* concert to a place of less gruesome associations.

Here is a house in a street off Tottenham Court Road. It is one of the stately-looking old houses that tell of a day when people of wealth and position lived around Fitzroy Square. These houses are now occupied as offices and warehouses, or let out in unfurnished floors.

In the front window of one of these houses hangs a card—"Apartments to Let." The vacant rooms are on the diningroom floor. Those two rooms were to let a year or two ago. One day the card was taken out of the window. A German lady had secured the apartments. She arrived about ten o'clock in the morning with her boxes and belongings on a van.

The vanmen unloaded the goods carefully and carried them in. They had great difficulty with one large trunk, and had to get assistance before they could put it into the back room. The heavy trunk plays a leading part in many of London's deepest mysteries.

A tall, slim, gentlemanly man, as soon as the box had disappeared into the house, strolled across the road, entered by the open door, and raised his hat to the German lady.

Madam bowed. The tall, slim gentleman was an old acquaintance. Madam had been useful to him on many occasions, supplying information which enabled him to discover the authors or authoresses of a good many robberies of a certain class. Madam was on the best terms with the police. "So you have moved from ———— Street?" said the detective.

"Yes, this morning."

"I've just come from ———— Street. What's been the matter in your place? One of the walls is smeared with blood."

"Really?" said Madam. "It must have been there a long time. Some furniture must have hidden it. I never noticed it."

"I see. Well, you are going to stay here for some time, I suppose?"

"Oh, yes, I hope so."

"Then why is that large trunk of yours addressed to 'The Station Master, Berlin—To be called for'?"

"I am sending some things there that I don't want."

"Oh! You might let me see what they are."

The detective went outside, gave an order to the vanmen, a knife was produced, the cords of the huge trunk were cut, and the lock forced. The lid sprang up, and the body of a man weighing eighteen stone was discovered inside. His skull had been split open with a hatchet.

The evidence brought forward at the trial saved Madam's neck by inducing the jury to make their verdict manslaughter. The sentence deprived the police of Madam's valuable information for twelve years.

We have looked up at the house in which Madam's secret was discovered; let us look at the house in which the crime was committed.

It is only a little distance away. Here is the street It has rather a Continental appearance. The names over the doors are mostly foreign. There is the house. Madam's room was on the first floor.

The first floor is to let. Plenty of people have occupied it since Madam gave it up. Some of them have slept night after night in the very room in which a man of eighteen stone was done to death, packed up in a trunk, and addressed to the station master at Berlin. Very few of the occupants, I fancy, have had any knowledge of the story of that room.

The tragedies pass and are forgotten. The houses of tragedy remain and are let to new tenants.

CHAPTER IX
LUNATICS AT LARGE

The Insanity of Crime—Lunatics without restraint—What happens at the end—A dangerous monster—A craze for killing—Why the crime was committed—Amiable lunatics—Children who are insane

IF to-morrow we were to read that the whole of the inmates of some great metropolitan lunatic asylum had escaped, and were still at large, the inhabitants of London would be seriously alarmed. There would be a general feeling of insecurity, for among the inmates of all great asylums there are many whose form of insanity is dangerous to the community, even when it is not the most serious form of all—homicidal mania.

And yet there are every day in London a sufficient number of lunatics in full possession of their liberty to fill one of its greatest asylums twice over, and many of them are homicidal maniacs.

Hardly a week passes that we do not read of some terrible act committed by a man or woman who has either been in an asylum or has a family history of insanity. But just before the tragedy these unfortunate people were moving about freely among their fellow-creatures, and all the time they were meditating murder, waiting for the opportunity to take a human life.

The series of diabolical crimes in the East End which appalled the world were committed by a homicidal maniac who led the ordinary life of a free citizen. He rode in tramcars and omnibuses. He travelled to Whitechapel by the underground railway, often late at night. Probably on several occasions he had but one fellow-passenger in the compartment with him, and that may have been a woman. Imagine what the feelings of those travellers would have been had they known that they were alone in the dark tunnels of the Underground with Jack the Ripper!

Some of us must have passed him in the street, sat with him perhaps at a café or a restaurant. He was a man of birth and education, and had sufficient means to keep himself without work. For a whole year at least he was a free man, exercising all the privileges of freedom. And yet he was a homicidal maniac of the most diabolical kind.

This horrible phase of insanity is not, fortunately, a common one. But there are maniacs of the Ripper type still at large. There have been several crimes of the Ripper character committed in low lodging-houses during recent years, and the perpetrator has always succeeded in making his escape and in retaining his liberty.

But the bulk of the dangerous lunatics at large are not systematic assassins. They are only wrought to frenzy by a fancied grievance or the stress of circumstance.

Many of the mysterious crimes of London which are apparently motiveless are the deeds of men who are insane on the subject of persecution. The victims of this form of delusion imagine that some person, often a public character or a celebrity constantly referred to in the Press, is secretly injuring them.

The murder of a popular actor some years ago was due to this cause. A man to whom he was an utter stranger imagined that the actor was keeping him out of an engagement, and he assassinated his imaginary enemy at the stage door of a West End theatre.

If a list could be prepared of the people against whom some lunatic at large has sworn to be revenged for a grievance which exists solely in the imagination of the aggressor, it would be a very alarming document.

It would show the world that a large number of men and women who are dangerously insane are living unrestrained lives, mixing with their fellow-citizens without let or hindrance, and only waiting for the opportunity to attack a supposed enemy.

Many of these people are looked upon by their acquaintances merely as cranks. After the Beck case I received hundreds of letters from people with a grievance; a large number of them were well written, and the addresses at the head of them showed that the writers were in a good position.

In some of these letters there was a threat of what would happen if the "persecutor" was not compelled by the Press to abandon his course of conduct. Some of them contained an unmistakable hint that murder might be the result if the persecution were not stopped or the wrong redressed.

And all these people, absolutely insane, were free from any sort of guardianship or control. Three of them called upon me.

One came late at night. He rushed in directly the door was opened and walked into my study, the door of which was open, before the astonished servant could interfere.

I saw at once what I had to deal with, and I listened with the greatest attention to the story my visitor had to tell. As he told it he worked himself up into a frenzy. His features became convulsed, and he struck my writing-table again and again with his clenched fist. I only got rid of him at last by recommending him to a firm of solicitors, who would take his case up and see that his enemy—a near relative—was legally restrained from conspiring with an oculist to put his eyes out.

Only once before have I conversed with a man who declaimed with such insane violence against an imagined enemy. I felt safer then, for the interview took place at Broadmoor, and two stalwart keepers stood by while the poor maniac foamed and raved.

A year after my visit to the Broadmoor patient—a gentleman whose case had excited a good deal of interest—there was a movement to obtain his release. His friends thought he was cured, and that it was quite safe for him to be restored to his family. Fortunately the authorities took a different view.

This gentleman had committed no actual crime. He had only pointed a pistol at the head of his "persecutor" and threatened to shoot him. Had he recovered in Broadmoor he would have been released. But his dementia had increased during his stay. The actual murderer who becomes sane leaves Broadmoor occasionally. It is not the King's pleasure to keep the sane in a lunatic asylum. In such cases every precaution is taken to insure control and comfort in the home to which the Broadmoor patient returns. The same care is not, unfortunately, always exercised by the authorities of non-criminal asylums, and every week scores of lunatics whose mental health has only been temporarily restored are discharged and return to the family and the home, and wander the streets of London at will.

The relative who is, or has been, in a lunatic asylum is the skeleton in many a family cupboard. In wealthy homes every care is taken to keep the mad member of the family under close observation, but among humble folks such care is impossible. The lunatic is left to look after himself.

There was a man hanged recently for murdering a relative. The murder was wanton and barbarous. The motive of it was a fancied grievance. No one came forward at the trial to save the murderer from the gallows. The barbarity of the crime had turned even his own relatives against him. But the accused had for ten years been looked upon as a madman in the neighbourhood in which he lived.

"He ought to be in an asylum," had been the criticism passed upon his conduct more than once.

Too late to save this man I ascertained the facts. "I've looked upon him as mad for years," said one of his neighbours to me, "and his people *knew* he was."

"Then why," I asked, "didn't they have him put under restraint?"

"Well, you see, he'd never murdered anybody before," was the reply.

That answer is typical of the public attitude towards lunatics at large. Unless they have killed or attempted to kill it is nobody's business to have them, in the interests of public safety, certified as insane.

We shudder at Caliban when we see him on the stage, and we tremble for Miranda. But there are dozens of Calibans in London, and they are free to roam where they like night and day.

Come down this court with me. Here is a monster deaf and dumb and deformed. Look at the hideous grimaces he makes, listen to the horrible sounds he utters. He is eight and twenty, and has lived in this court for ten years with his mother and father. #

The children tease him. Occasionally they irritate him to such an extent that with a series of wild howls he rushes at them. Then they run away, and presently an aged woman will come out of her home in the court and coax Caliban into a good humour, and lead him indoors. The aged woman is Caliban's mother—she cannot be always looking after him, because she has to make cardboard boxes for a living.

Some day there will be a terrible crime committed in that court, or Caliban will wander away to do his deed, and there will be a shocking story in the newspapers. Then everyone will wonder why Caliban was not put in an asylum where he could be properly guarded and restrained. He is a monster, likely to commit a brutal crime at any moment. But as he has not, so far, done anything criminal, no one thinks it worth while to limit the bounds of his freedom.

Some of the mysterious crimes which baffle the police, because they can find no "motive" to give them a clue, are the deeds of homicidal maniacs at large. The crimes are often committed without provocation. The victim is unknown to them. The opportunity of killing occurs, and it is eagerly seized. Then the maniac, if he has escaped observation, goes quietly home, and thinks no more of his deed. In some cases he has no further knowledge of it.

I spent an afternoon in his private apartment at Broadmoor some time ago with a highly-cultured gentleman who left his chambers late one night, went out on to the Embankment, sat down on a seat on which a tramp was sleeping, and deliberately murdered the tramp. He shot him with a revolver. People hearing the shot ran up, and the murderer was arrested. But if he had throttled the man or stabbed him he would have gone quietly home again, and the murder would have remained a mystery.

When the prisoner was questioned the next day he had no recollection of what had occurred. He couldn't understand why he was detained. This unfortunate gentleman had a large circle of friends and acquaintances, many of whom had been his guests at the pleasant little dinner-parties he used to give in his luxurious chambers. None of them had the slightest suspicion that he was insane.

Nor would anyone suspect it who conversed with him to-day at Broadmoor. As a matter of fact, he is perfectly sane until midnight. But at midnight his entire nature changes, and he has to be approached with the greatest caution. From midnight till the break of day he is a maniac with a desire to kill. After that he is an amiable and cultured gentleman with whom it is a pleasure to associate.

One of the most charming men I ever met, a man so benevolent in appearance, so gentle in manner, that it seems to me even now impossible to think of him as a murderer, waited with a revolver night after night to kill a young fellow against whom he had an imaginary grievance. He succeeded at last. He shot his "enemy" dead at the corner of a street, and then walked quietly away. When he was seized he explained that he had only performed an act of justice, and he requested his captors to release him. He was anxious to get home at once, as he had friends coming to supper.

Had no one been about to see the murder, this genial old gentleman would have gone home to his little supper-party and played the host to perfection. His "persecutor" settled with, he would probably have lived a quiet and gentle life for the remainder of his days. The "stress" being removed he might have become sane, and in his sanity he would have forgotten all about the murder he had committed.

The lunatic at large may commit murder at any time, or he may go to the end of his days without doing the slightest harm to anyone. The merest accident may stir the smouldering fire to flame. The unfortunate barmaid who was discovered murdered in a railway carriage at Waterloo Station with a bloodstained pestle was, it is believed, the victim of her resemblance to another young woman.

The theory of this crime, which still remains a mystery, is that the victim was killed by a young man who had been jilted by a girl to whom he was devotedly attached. The disappointment in love affected the man's brain. One night he entered a railway carriage, and, finding himself seated opposite the living image of the woman who had broken his heart, roused to madness by the sight of *that face*, he fiercely attacked the unfortunate young woman who was alone with him. Why, if the murder was not *planned*, he had a pestle with him, need not be argued. Whoever the murderer was he could not have calculated at the time he armed himself with a weapon that he would find himself alone with his victim in a railway carriage. The police suspected various persons at first, but later on obtained evidence which pointed strongly in the direction I have indicated. But this evidence was not sufficient to justify the suspected person being brought to trial.

Lunatics at large are not always unpleasant people; some of them are exceedingly amiable. Their amiability is, however, apt to be embarrassing. A popular tragedian who, on certain occasions, was in the habit of having wreaths handed to him across the footlights, once told me of a painful experience. An elderly lady who admired him exceedingly, determined to make him a few wreaths herself and present them to him in private life. She found out where he lived, and watched his front door. As he came out into the street she would step forward with a smile and slip a home-made wreath over his head. The tragedian didn't want to hurt the poor old lady's feelings by flinging it away, so he took it off and walked to the corner of the street with it in his hand, and then hailed a cab and drove to the theatre.

After that the old lady waylaid him almost every week, and wanted to cover him with flowers. She did succeed one day in slipping a chain of wild flowers about his neck. The great actor became nervous. He couldn't ask the police to protect him against an amiable old lady, and he didn't care to denounce her as a lunatic for considering him worthy of wreaths and garlands. Fortunately for his peace of mind the persecution suddenly ceased. What became of the old lady he never knew.

There was a dear old lady once who made me very unhappy. She lived close to me in Regent's Park, and every day she called at my house and left a few daisies or buttercups, or a handful of simple flowers. That was very nice, but when she began to stand in front of my door and make little speeches about me, scattering floral offerings on my doorstep, and putting buttercups and daisies into my letter-box, I began to feel uncomfortable. One day she went into a flower-shop in Baker Street and ordered garlands of flowers to be sent up and twined about my railings. Fortunately the lady at the flower-shop saw that the dear old soul was not right in her mind, and didn't execute the order. Some weeks after I heard that the old lady had been taken away to an asylum.

This was an agreeable form of madness; much more agreeable than the form insanity took with a young man for whom—believing the tale he told me to be true—I bought a cornet. He assured me that he could earn his living with it, and keep his poor old father and mother out of the workhouse. He came outside my house every night late—sometimes at one and two in the morning—and played that comet. And he played it very badly.

It was only after I had put someone on to follow the comet-player to his home that I discovered that he was in perfectly good circumstances—independent circumstances, in fact—but imagined that he was poor and earning his living as a street musician. He had been in a lunatic asylum for eighteen months, and had only left it a fortnight when he came to me.

Some years ago a madman took a fancy to me, with a much more painful result. He wrote me the most extraordinary letters, to which at first I replied, but I very soon discovered that my correspondent was a violent lunatic, and

I ceased to acknowledge his effusions. This made no difference. They poured in upon me as freely as ever.

One day he wrote to me and enclosed the ticket of a travelling bag which he had left at Charing Cross. "I shall commit suicide to-night," he said in the letter; "I have left you my jewellery and all my securities. You will find them in the bag at Charing Cross. I enclose you the ticket for it."

When I opened my "Daily Telegraph" I found that my correspondent had carried out his threat. He had shot himself—fortunately not fatally—in Regent Street the previous evening. I gave the ticket of the bag to the police, who handed it over to the poor fellow's relatives. The bag contained jewellery and securities to the value of many hundreds of pounds.

A painful feature in this phase of London life is the large number of children who are not in possession of their mental faculties, and yet are not under any proper control. Of the little boy who murders a baby brother or sister we hear occasionally. Of the child who only *attempts* to murder we hear rarely. But the schools for the feeble-minded which are now established in every part of London have a large number of dangerous children of both sexes passing daily from and to their homes and enjoying the full liberties of life in the streets.

This is not the place in which to set forth the terrible dangers to which society will presently be exposed by the ever-increasing numbers of mental and physical degenerates for whose detention, after a certain age, no provision is made by the State.

But before this series is concluded I may, with all due discretion, lift a portion of the veil and give my readers some slight insight into one of the most disquieting phases of life in this great city of packed and seething humanity.

It is not a phase which can be ignored, for statistics show us that the feeble-minded and the insane are increasing at a rate which is entirely out of proportion to the rate of increase in the population.

For every lunatic at large to-day we shall have—unless legislation finds a means of minimizing and dealing with the evil—five lunatics at large in ten years' time.

And it is to lunatics at large that we owe some of the most gruesome, the most appalling Mysteries of modern London.

CHAPTER X
"FROM INFORMATION RECEIVED"

Secret stories of spies—How Royalty is protected—A scare—Criminals are afraid of women—A traitor who was murdered—How evidence is discovered—Confessors who hold their peace

SCATTERED over London is a small army of spies and informers, men and women, whose business—sometimes whose pleasure—it is to make communications to the authorities with regard to their fellow-citizens. The romance of the Government spy or secret service agent is one thing; the romance of the police informer or "nark" is another.

The spies of foreign Governments are of all classes. Some of them belong to West End clubs and fare sumptuously every day; others are of humble appearance and menial occupation. The spies of Russia are popularly supposed to be highly interesting personalities. Furnished with substantial funds and first-class introductions, they mix with the best society, and have the *entrée* of the most exclusive circles.

But the Russian spy is in Soho and in Whitechapel, as well as in Mayfair and Belgravia, and some of the most active are members of the revolutionary societies which have their West End meetings in a club near Fitzroy Square, W.C., and their East End meetings in a club near Brick Lane, Spitalfields.

Germany and France have their spies and secret service agents in London, and some of them are British subjects who are taking foreign pay to assist in the betrayal of their country's secrets.

The days are gone when foreign Governments subsidized London newspapers; but every foreign Government of importance has in London its secret representatives, and men and women who are practically members of its secret police.

Some of these people are suspected, some of them are known, but the majority go about their business so skilfully that no one, not even their most intimate friend, has any idea of the nature of their real occupation or the real source of their income.

The stories that might be written of the foreign spies of London are many. The stories that will be written are few. There are certain diplomatic considerations which make official silence imperative, even when suspicion has developed into absolute certainty.

We do not suffer from the spy mania here as they do in France. We do not suspect the foreign tourist who arrives with a camera of designs upon our fortifications; and in our easy-going way we credit foreign Governments, especially Germany, with knowing already quite as much about our national defences as we do ourselves. With the spies who are over here looking after foreign political offenders who have sought "asylum" in the capital we have no concern. In this free land they are as free as the men whose actions they are watching, whose footsteps they are dogging, and whose fate they are seeking to encompass.

We know that London is the centre of the revolutionary movements of Europe. We know that here most of the assassinations which have shocked the world have been plotted and planned. The name and place of abode of every foreign anarchist who comes to this country are registered at Scotland Yard. The system of observation is as perfect as can be, and valuable information is constantly given to the foreign Governments as to the movements of suspected individuals. But the anarchists live in safety and plot in security. It is not our custom to take violent measures against them. To this policy we owe the immunity from outrage that we enjoy. The anarchists of Europe have no desire to make themselves objectionable in England. "Leave us alone and we will leave you alone" is the unwritten understanding in "Red" London between the foreign revolutionaries and the authorities.

There was a time when the apostles of the infernal machine and the bomb sought to terrify our own Government, and then the tension at the Yard was terrible. Spies and informers there were who brought news of many a plot and prevented its accomplishment; but every now and then the dastardly design was carried out. That time is happily passed, and the "Reds" only cause the heads of the police extra anxiety when some foreign potentate is visiting our King and driving openly through the streets of London.

On these occasions every foreign anarchist and terrorist known to the police—and I doubt if there is one in our midst who is not—is shadowed. Some of them may get into a house on the line of procession; some of them may mix with the crowd.

But wherever they are there is someone at their elbow who is watching every movement, ready at the first hint of danger to act promptly and decisively.

When recently the King of Spain drove through the streets of London I stood in the crowd close to a foreign anarchist who makes violent speeches in a certain "Red" club in a back street in Soho. He was so closely wedged in between two stalwart-looking men of the navvy type that when the King of Spain came by he, the anarchist, couldn't have got his hands up to take off his hat had he wanted to do so. The navvies were police officers.

On the occasion of the present Tsar's last visit to London as the Cesarewitch the precautions taken were of an extraordinary character. The anarchists and

Russian terrorists in London were not only closely watched, but they were prevented from getting close to the line of route or near to the Royal Palaces.

The known revolutionaries are easy to deal with. The police have daily information of their movements. The "cranks" are the real terror of the authorities, for you never know what a crank will do.

A pale-faced, middle-aged woman in black, caused considerable consternation by attempting to enter St. James's Palace with a suspicious-looking box. She was promptly seized by the police.

On the box being opened with every precaution, under the impression that it was an infernal machine, it was found to contain a long steel chain and a letter to the Cesarewitch, calling his attention to the fact that chains of this description were being worn by the Russian Jews in Siberia. The whole thing was harmless enough, but the officials who first saw that box had a very bad moment.

On every occasion of the visit of a foreign potentate in London the "information" received is of voluminous character. Some of it is worth serious consideration, but a good deal of it is of the "crank" order, with just enough appearance of sanity in it to cause the authorities considerable trouble and anxiety.

The "information received" with regard to ordinary crimes and ordinary criminals is of a different kind. The information on which the police as a rule act when they obtain a "clue" to a mystery is furnished from outside. Sometimes it comes from an acquaintance of the guilty person—as often as not, when the guilty person is a professional criminal, it comes from a jealous woman or from a "nark"—that is, from a person who mixes with a criminal set as one of themselves, and is all the time in constant communication with the police.

"From information I received I went to such and such an address," is the conventional opening of the police officer's evidence.

Very rarely does the real source of information transpire. For the police to give away a professional informer would be to lose an important ally in their war against crime. The deputy of a low lodging-house, the landlord of a public-house frequented by bad characters, would have to pay a heavy penalty if it were known that he was the person who told the police where to put their hand on the "wanted" man. Still worse would it fare with the women who, often when the proceeds of the job have been spent upon them, give Scotland Yard the "office" that So-and-so has been flush of money ever since the night of a certain burglary or shop robbery.

Some of the most expert criminals in London always work single-handed. They might trust a "pal," but they mistrust a pal's pal, and they are especially prejudiced against his female acquaintances. In nine cases out of ten it is a woman who has given the first information to Scotland Yard when a professional criminal who has covered his tracks with the greatest success is suddenly pounced upon by an active and intelligent officer.

Sometimes the betrayal is due to a quarrel in which the woman has been badly knocked about; sometimes it is due to jealousy, but as often as not the information comes from a woman who lives in the neighbourhood, who consorts with thieves, who is herself the wife or the sweetheart of a criminal, but is at the same time a spy acting for the police and in receipt of police pay.

The subject is one upon which it is necessary to write with discretion. In the interests of justice a certain reticence is imperative in such a matter as this. If it were not so I might show how in some sensational cases which have recently been tried the guilty persons would never have been brought to justice but for an act of betrayal which was treacherous in the extreme.

When one knows who committed a murder, to conceal that knowledge is to be an accessory after the fact. The law demands that the knowledge shall instantly be placed at the service of the police. I am not considering information given with regard to murder as treacherous. The cases I have in my mind are those in which the crime was incited by certain individuals who for purposes of their own intended to betray the criminal.

The "*agent provocateur*" the person who incites a fellow-citizen to commit a crime in order that the police may make a clever capture or secure a dangerous criminal who has hitherto evaded their well-spread net, is not, fortunately, a conventional character in the British judicial drama.

But there are men and women who put up burglaries and robberies and criminal schemes in order that they may give information and get their victims caught in the act.

Not long ago a young policeman captured a man with a quantity of silver plate in his possession. The man was coming from a house in the suburbs at an early hour in the morning.

When the man was brought before the magistrate he told in self-defence a most extraordinary story. He was an ex-convict, but he was leading an honest life and working under the police. He called a police officer as a witness on his behalf, and the officer acknowledged that the man's story was correct.

The prisoner had given information that a burglary was to be committed, and had, "in the interests of justice," taken part in it himself. When he was captured he was on his way to take the stolen property to the police-station, and the information he had given had enabled the authorities to secure the other men. "The prisoner was discharged." If you read between the lines of this story you will have a fair idea of the way in which the professional "nark" works in connection with what—at least, so far as he is concerned—is a put-up job—a trap deliberately arranged for the capture of a criminal.

When a sensational crime has been committed by confederates or by a "gang," and the hue and cry continues unabated, it sometimes happens that one of them tries to make himself safe by offering information to the authorities on certain well-under-stood conditions.

"King's evidence" is recognized as a necessary evil, for it is occasionally the only evidence upon which a conviction could possibly be obtained. Turning King's evidence does not always save the traitor. He may escape the punishment of the law, only to meet with a tragic fate at other hands. Carey, one of the informers at the Phoenix Park murder trial, was got safely away, only to be shot dead by Patrick O'Donell on board a steamship near Port Elizabeth, South Africa.

Other informers less notorious met with "fatal accidents" in far-off lands. Two who went to Paris and lived under assumed names came to the Morgue. They were "found drowned" in the Seine.

The informer in the great bank-note forgery case was doomed to death by the men whom he had betrayed. The revolver with which the elder Barmash committed suicide after sentence had been passed upon him was intended to be used upon the informer who stood in the dock a fellow-prisoner. The opportunity of shooting him did not occur. The man was never in a position in which he could be safely aimed at.

But the informer is not always called upon to make a public appearance. Many of the tales we read about the marvellous discovery of a clue by the police would be shorn of their romance if we knew that an important fact was being kept in the background—viz. that the detective in charge of the investigation had received a communication informing him exactly where to look for the incriminating piece of evidence.

Sometimes the information is anonymous. A few words scribbled on half a sheet of notepaper brought two men to the gallows. The writer suggested that a visit should be paid to a certain house where a little boy would be found who had lost a toy. The hint was taken, and the tale the child told of his missing toy led to one of the most sensational captures of modern times.

Nothing was said about the information that furnished the police with the clue. There was no necessity to tell the story, or to produce the anonymous letter. Yet, but for that hint, it is probable that the crime would have remained one of the unfathomed mysteries of the Metropolis.

A year or two ago a foreign woman was tried for murder. The evidence—although the body of her victim had been concealed in a trunk—justified a verdict of manslaughter, and the woman only got a term of penal servitude.

For two years this woman had been of the greatest assistance to justice. She had become associated with a dangerous class of women in a West End district, and when a man had been robbed by one of them, or by men acting in concert with them, this foreign woman made it her business to find out who the guilty parties were, and to send their names to the police.

She was to all intents and purposes a police spy living the life of the class upon whom she was spying, and for certain reasons enjoying their confidence.

The professional informer or "nark" is rarely suspected. Personal communication with the authorities is avoided as much as possible. Sometimes, in order to put a desperate gang off the scent, the spy who has been in close relationship with them is arrested too, and discharged on account of "insufficient evidence" to implicate him.

To the student of humanity even more interesting than the professional informers are the honest people who become possessed of information with regard to criminal deeds, and from conscientious motives hold their peace.

The Roman Catholic clergy never, of course, betray that which they learn under the seal of confession. But it sometimes happens that terrible secrets are learnt by Protestant clergymen, Salvation Army workers, doctors, and nurses.

A fierce press discussion raged some years ago around the action of a Salvation Army captain to whom a crime was confessed by a penitent, and who went straight away and gave information. Some people held that the action was justified, others that the confession was made in circumstances which did not justify its betrayal.

After the conviction of Israel Lipski for the murder of a Jewess in the East End there was considerable doubt as to his guilt. It looked for a time as if he was likely to be reprieved. A Jewish Rabbi, to whom Lipski had already confessed, kept the secret inviolate until the Home Secretary had refused the petition. The Rabbi knew the man was guilty, but he felt he had no right to use his confession against him.

The secrets of many of the mysteries which have baffled the police are in the possession of men and women who for one motive or another hesitate to reveal them.

The reason for silence is sometimes relationship to the guilty person. A wife cannot be expected to give her husband to the gallows, a father or mother cannot be expected to speak the word which would send a son to a shameful death.

So all the time they keep the ghastly secret and live in constant terror that some day the truth may be discovered.

But most criminals are "given away" sooner or later by informers. How many are thus handed over to justice the public have no means of estimating. The police rule is to screen the "nark" at all hazards. The moment an informer is put in the witness-box his value as an instrument in the detection of crime is destroyed for ever.

The system is absolutely necessary. After the commission of an offence supposed to be the work of a professional criminal, the detective department must know where it can obtain accurate information as to the latest movements of the men likely to have been concerned. It does know. There is scarcely a criminal on the police books who is not kept under observation by one of his own class who "for a consideration" will betray him.

CHAPTER XI
THE MYSTERY OF MONEY SPENT

Murder for a few shillings—living on their wits—The value of a handshake—Where the money came from—The mystery of a large income—Price of a lost letter—An unwelcome burglar

ONE half of the world does not know how the other half lives." That is a stock phrase which has been worn threadbare by over-use. And if you analyse it, it appears so self-evident that one wonders at the daring of the person who first put it forward as an original observation. Very few people really know how their next-door neighbours live. They may think they do, but they are often entirely wrong in the conclusion they have arrived at.

One of the great mysteries of a vast city is how all the people in it manage to get a living. If you take a day of London life, apart from its work, and consider the hundreds of thousands of people who are merely amusing themselves and spending collectively a sum of money in the process which, if put in round figures, would astound you, you are faced with a greater mystery still.

Who are the people who during the working hours of the day can assemble in their tens of thousands at the popular race-meetings, the great cricket-matches, the afternoon performances at the theatres, the Palaces of Variety, the concert-rooms, the exhibitions, and the side-shows?

I never see a great match at Lord's or at the Oval and look around at the packed masses of spectators without wondering how the great majority arrange to have the leisure on a working day, and how some of them manage to have the price of admission to spare.

It would be a wild flight of imagination to suppose that to get the money to attend a cricket match some of the spectators had committed a crime. And yet, a few years ago, two little boys paid their sixpence each at the pay-box at Lord's and passed in, enjoyed the game, applauded the big hits, and in the evening went back to the room in which their mother lay dead, and slept in it, tired out with the day's enjoyment.

These little boys were shortly afterwards, owing to certain suspicious circumstances, arrested, and they then confessed that their mother being ill in bed they had murdered her in order to rob her of a few shillings. It was with a portion of this money they had spent a happy day at Lord's watching a cricket match.

It is a gruesome idea to associate with cricket, but the trail of tragedy passes even over the green patch on which the national pastime is played.

I have in my possession the last letter a well-known groundsman ever wrote. It was written in the condemned cell in Bedford Gaol the night before his execution. The last words of that letter, written as a P.S. after the unhappy man's signature, are "No more cricket."

Who that sat near those two little boys as they cheered a boundary hit would have thought that they had that morning murdered their mother? Who that saw this unfortunate groundsman bowling at the nets to some famous batsman of the day would have imagined that he was shortly to end his life on the gallows for cruelly and deliberately murdering his young wife and her mother?

One of the spectators at a great football match at the Crystal Palace was Alfred Stratton, the "mask" murderer. He paid his fare and his admission money to the football ground with the cash he had obtained by killing Mr. and Mrs. Farrow.

As we sit in the packed theatre or music-hall, or mix with the crowd on the race-course, to how many of us does it present itself as a probability that some of the people present are enjoying themselves with money obtained by murder?

Here is a well-known West End café. In the same building is a restaurant. The best people in London are among the frequenters of both. The company present when we enter is not of a kind to excite the slightest suspicion in our minds. The natural assumption is that they are all good citizens of unimpeachable character, and that the money they are spending is legitimately theirs.

But, looking round the crowded room, I can, from my own personal knowledge of facts, select half a dozen specimens of the mystery of the money spent.

A tall, military-looking man leaves one of the tables as we enter and comes across and shakes hands with me.

It would be rude of me to say "I don't know you" in a public room. He sees my hesitation and exclaims, "Ah! you don't remember me, I see. I am Sir — —————. I used to see you very often at the old Pelican Club."

I make a conventional reply and pass to the other end of the room. My impression of Sir ————— is not a favourable one.

I remember having heard something about him, and I am a little uneasy at this public claiming of acquaintanceship. The Baronet is with a lady—a very charming lady, to judge by her appearance. I ask an *habitué* of the café, who is a friend of mine, if he knows anything about Sir —————.

"I don't think much of him," is the reply. "He was here with that lady the day before yesterday, and he got up and shook hands with Colonel ———— — just as he did with you. The Colonel told me afterwards he was sure he had never met the man before."

Two weeks later the reason for this little comedy of acquaintanceship was made clear. The Baronet appeared at Bow Street police court and turned out to be no baronet at all, but an adventurer who had imposed his title upon confiding tradespeople and unsuspecting women. He had victimized half a dozen of the former and married two of the latter. And from both he had obtained a considerable amount of money.

Sir ———— got his living by frequenting the haunts of well-known people, shaking hands with some of them, and so establishing himself in the confidence of his dupes, one or other of whom he was in the habit of inviting to lunch at the restaurant and to sit in the café with him afterwards.

The "trick" is not a new one. A high police official whose features are well known once told me of a case in which he had been selected for the "old acquaintance" dodge. A gentleman in a restaurant came up to the official and shook him warmly by the hand. "Ah! my dear ————. How are you?" he said in a loud voice. "I hope Mrs. ———— is better."

The official's wife *had* been very ill, and the question at once disarmed him. He returned the hand-shake, imagining that the man really *was* an acquaintance whose face he failed to recall.

On the strength of that hand-shake the "acquaintance" succeeded in victimizing a gentleman who witnessed the interview to the extent of £500. A high police official would hardly shake hands in a public place with a swindler.

But let us take another look round the café in which the sham Baronet claimed acquaintance with me.

At a table in the far corner three smartly-dressed men are seated. They are smoking the most expensive cigars and drinking the oldest liqueur brandy in the establishment.

To them there enters presently an elegantly-dressed lady. She is past her first youth and is inclining to stoutness, but she is still attractive, and her manners are perfect.

The three men rise and salute her with almost Continental effusiveness. They address her as "Countess." Presently the little party of friends are conversing earnestly together, but in an undertone, as is the custom with people in good society who talk together in a place of public resort.

The three men are accomplished and clever rascals. One of them is a card-sharper of "distinction," another has made blackmailing a fine art. The third is a solicitor who has not yet been struck off the rolls. The lady is a "Monte Carlo Countess"; it is possible that she may have been married at one time of her life to a Polish Count, but her present occupation is that of a professional *fiancée*. The solicitor at the little table has settled three breaches of promise for her without any of them coming into court. Both in this matter and in the little parties which the Countess gives at her luxuriously-furnished flat the other gentlemen at the table are exceedingly useful to her. It is needless to add they receive their share of the stakes for bringing down the bird which the Countess "puts up."

In the days when the Vaudeville was a burlesque house a popular burlesque actress appearing there became engaged to a young gentleman who was lavish in his generosity in the matter of presents. He hardly allowed a week to pass without giving her some costly article of jewellery.

The sudden wealth of this young gentleman astonished Mr. Robert Reece, the author of the burlesque, who had known him as a clerk in a West-end bill discounter's office. Mr. Reece spoke to the young actress and begged her to make sure of her *fiancées* position and prospects before she married him.

She had no necessity to act on this advice, as the very next evening the young gentleman was arrested while waiting at the stage door for her. He was accused of having forged and discounted bills to the amount of £15,000. His legitimate earnings at the time he was making the young lady such costly presents amounted to £3 a week. In her dressing-room at the Vaudeville Theatre the actress handed over to the police all the jewellery she had received. It was valued in court at several thousand pounds.

The sudden possession of funds by a thief known to the police always attracts their unpleasant attention. Such a man must carefully avoid ostentation in his own neighbourhood. He does not even risk changing a sovereign in the public-houses that he "uses" lest the action should be observed by a "nark."

But there is a class of more or less "shady" individuals who, being habitually in possession of money, can indulge in extra extravagance without running any extra risk.

The Bogus Charity Collecting Brigade has all classes in its ranks. There are men and women of decent appearance, good manners, and good education, who make this form of fraud their means of livelihood. They have no other occupation and no other source of income, and every penny of the money they spend in food, clothing, and rent, is earned by false pretences. But it is only those who practise frauds upon the benevolent upon a large scale, live luxuriously on the proceeds, and generally, sooner or later, find themselves the subject of a personal memoir in "Truth," who are interesting to the public.

When a director of the Great Northern Railway saw a peer shake hands at a railway station with a man whom the director knew to be a clerk in the company's office he was astonished. He was considerably more astonished when the peer explained that the friend he had just greeted gave the best dinners in London.

It was that accidental meeting that brought the famous Red-path forgeries to light.

The mystery of the money spent disappeared when a well-dressed, well-groomed gentleman came up the steps into the dock at Clerkenwell Police Court.

I knew a man for twenty years who was respected and beloved by a wide circle of friends. He was an unostentatious man, but he had a beautiful house, he spent large sums in collecting works of art, and his benevolence was unbounded. He was secretary to a charitable institution, but it was supposed that he only retained the office because he loved the work.

The salary was a small one, but that did not matter. He had acquired riches by marrying a wealthy wife. He married this wealthy lady when he was five-and-thirty, and he was over sixty when he was one day called out of his dining-room just as he was sitting down to entertain a large party of friends, and failed to return.

His wife, who had taken her seat at the table, was sent for a minute or two after her husband had quitted the company, and she also failed to return.

The guests sat for a time, wondering what had happened. They wondered still more when a servant came back with a message that Mr. ——— had received a very important communication which compelled him to ask his guests to quit the house.

The next day the wealthy secretary of the charitable institution appeared at the police-court, and the evening papers contained the statement that he was charged with having robbed the institution of over sixty thousand pounds, the defalcations extending over a number of years.

At the trial it was elicited that the lady he had married was a young woman to whom he had been left guardian, and that he had spent every farthing of her money before he proposed to her, and made her his wife in order to cover up his crime.

Some years ago I knew a man who used to hang about racecourses and outside certain sporting clubs when any sporting event was on. He had a bad record, and used it to get his living. If, on a race-course, you lost a valuable article of jewellery—a gold watch or a diamond pin, or something valued for its associations—this man could generally be relied upon to trace it and get it back "at a price."

I saw him one night loafing about outside a sporting club, evidently hard up. A year later I saw him in fine feather and quite the "sporting gent.," as he would have said, at Nice races, and that night I met him again in evening dress at the roulette tables at Monte Carlo. He was living luxuriously at one of the best hotels. I met him a year or two later in a railway carriage coming back from Newmarket after the Cambridgeshire, and I gathered from his conversation with another passenger that he was going to try Egypt for his winter trip.

The "mystery of the money spent" in this case was not to be accounted for by any sudden stroke of luck on the Turf. The man had a good, solid income which enabled him to live at ease all the year round. His change of fortune dated from the day he was put on to try and recover a pocket-book which had been stolen from the rooms of an exceedingly wealthy young man, well known in sporting circles.

The pocket-book was recovered, with the bank-notes which it had contained missing, but a certain letter which the owner had placed in it still there. The letter must have been a very important one. The bargain struck for its restoration started the restorer on the road to fortune.

A professional burglar—a man who had been a skilled mechanic, earning good wages, in early life, but had taken to evil ways—broke into a West End mansion in the small hours. It happened that the tenant of the mansion had been making a very late night of it with some friends, and, entering his house with his latchkey at 4 a.m., he came upon the burglar in the dining-room.

The next morning the burglar went to the tenement house in which he was living with his wife, flung a handful of gold into her lap, told her to go and buy herself some good clothes while he went and got himself decently rigged out. She was to meet him in the afternoon at a given place. The husband and wife met, well dressed, and set out to look for a villa residence in the suburbs. They took a nice house, furnished it elegantly, if somewhat showily, engaged servants, and settled down into easy suburban well-to-do-ness. They had a horse and trap, and were looked upon by their neighbours as retired tradespeople, who had made their money and were living on a well-earned competency.

The ex-burglar and his wife enjoyed themselves. They had an occasional week at Brighton, or Margate, or Yarmouth; and in the summer they went away for a month or six weeks.

How did their change of fortune come? How did a burglar who was so badly off that he lived with his wife in one room in a tenement house suddenly develop into a well-to-do retired tradesman with plenty of money to spend?

The secret of the sudden access of wealth lay in the chance meeting of the burglar and the burgled in that West End mansion.

The tenant was a man of fifty, who had recently returned with a large fortune from South Africa. When he found a burglar on his premises he seized him by the throat. But as the light fell upon his assailant the burglar uttered a cry, not of terror, but of astonishment.

"Jack!" he exclaimed.

Five minutes later the two men were quietly discussing the new situation.

Twenty years previously they had met in a convict prison, where both were undergoing punishment—one for breaking into a jeweller's shop, the other for embezzling the money of his employer. They had been "pals" in prison, and had remained pals for a time after their liberation.

The burglar continued in his evil courses, but the clerk, getting assistance from some relatives, went out to South Africa. Being a ticket-of-leave man who had neglected to report himself at Scotland Yard, he was liable to be arrested on his return and sent back to prison to complete the remitted portion of his sentence. He had taken a new name in South Africa, and in this new name had made his fortune.

The police were not likely to associate the wealthy tenant of the West End mansion with the ex-convict who had failed to observe the terms of his license, and he was safe. That is to say, he was safe until the burglar who had broken into his house recognized him.

The silence of the old fellow "lag" was worth a good deal to the millionaire, and he paid it. This is how the ex-burglar was able to settle down as a respectable citizen in a pretty villa residence and deny himself nothing in the way of comfort or enjoyment.

Hush-money as a source of income is not confined to the class we usually associate with it. There are plenty of men and women moving in what is called good society who find it a profitable occupation to hold their tongue.

CHAPTER XII
THE UNKNOWN FATE

Motives for disappearance—Was he John Sadleir?—Swallowed up— A tragedy that came to light—How a body can be disposed of— Startling evidence—The ease of a secret burial

EVERY year a certain number of men and women disappear suddenly from their homes, from their accustomed haunts, from the circle of their friends and acquaintances. Without cause, without any reason that can be surmised, they vanish; and the fate of many of them remains an unsolved mystery to the last.

Scarcely a week passes that the newspaper reader does not see the headline "Mysterious disappearance." Now and again it is a man of mature age, married, the father of a family, and in good circumstances. But more frequently it is a young woman.

A large number of these disappearances are soon accounted for, thanks to the vast circulation of our modern newspapers and their custom of reproducing a photograph of the missing person.

The young woman who disappears from London is discovered living quietly at the seaside or in some provincial town. The fact that Miss So-and-so has been found is duly chronicled, and the public trouble no more about the matter.

The mystery has probably been no mystery at all to the relatives of the wanderer. In some cases melancholia, in others a family disagreement, has preceded the foolish act. Disappointment in love, or unhappiness at home, occasionally financial embarrassment, has been the cause of the adventure. These are the ordinary, everyday disappearances, which mean only the waywardness or the wilfulness of the individual.

But the number of disappearances which justify the use in every sense of the word "mysterious" is still great. A man drops suddenly out of life. He was, and in a moment he is not. He has vanished as though by magic, and there is nothing to indicate that the act of disappearance has been a voluntary one.

The desire to disappear, to drop a life that has its embarrassments, its unpleasantnesses, its limitations, may come to many of us; but there are generally circumstances which make the accomplishment of the desire exceedingly difficult. We are chained by a set of circumstances from which it is impossible to free ourselves without incurring consequences which may be disastrous, not only to ourselves, but to those we leave in ignorance of our fate.

After calamities in which there has been great loss of life and difficulty in identifying some of the victims, there are always a certain number of people who avail themselves of the opportunity of having their fate conjectured, and never return to their homes.

So it comes about that husbands and wives are mourned as dead, their names, it may be, recorded upon the memorial stone above the family tomb, who are still in the land of the living. Under other names, far from the chance of recognition, they are living new lives with new family ties to replace the old ones they suddenly severed.

That is the mystery of the dead alive, a fascinating subject upon which many a romance has been written. To this day there are people who believe the astounding story told by men who affirmed that they had met Fauntleroy in America after his execution, and it was for a long time the custom to explain that this marvel had happened through the unfortunate banker being hanged with a silver tube in his throat.

On the popular belief that John Sadleir, Member for Sligo, a Junior Lord of the Treasury, Chairman of the London Joint Stock Banking Company, and the most successful swindler of modern times, obtained the body of a man resembling himself, conveyed it to Hampstead Heath, and placed his own silver cream jug with the remains of poison in it beside the corpse, Miss Braddon founded one of her famous novels.

The fact that gave rise to the doubt as to Sadleir's being really dead was this: The body of the supposed Sadleir was found on Hampstead Heath some distance from the roadway or path. It had been a rainy evening, and the heath was sodden. But the soles of the boots the dead man was wearing were clean and unstained with moisture.

Sadleir did not leave his house till nearly midnight, long after the heavy rain had commenced. How did he cross the heath and lie down to poison himself and die without wetting the soles of his boots?

This strange circumstance was recalled when, long after the witnesses before the coroner's jury had identified the body as that of Sadleir, three men who had known him well declared that they had met him on the other side of the Atlantic.

In these instances of the dead alive there is only vague surmise to grasp at. The element of a grim certainty enters into the cases of those who drop out of life to meet an unascertained fate.

A friend of mine—an artist with whom in bygone years it was my privilege to be associated—had a daughter, a charming and beautiful girl of eighteen. She had no love affair or trouble of any kind. One winter evening about seven o'clock her mother wanted some Berlin wool. Close by the house was a shopping street where the wool could be obtained. The girl offered to fetch it for her mother, and went out with a shilling or two in her pocket.

She bought the wool, but she never came back with it. From that hour to this—an interval of seven years—no living soul who knew that beautiful girl has ever set eyes on her again. Every effort to trace her has been in vain. She was seen at the end of the shopping street by a neighbour making her way towards her home. But between the end of that street and the house whose doors she was never to enter again she dropped out of human ken for ever.

One day a man whom I knew—a prosperous suburban tradesman—went into a City office—the office of a firm with whom he had business transactions. He paid an account, and said he should come back late in the afternoon to give an order. He was going to his bank to cash a cheque.

He was seen within a few hundred yards of that bank by an acquaintance, but he never cashed the cheque, and he was never heard of again. For fifteen years his widow refused to abandon hope. She always thought that one day he would come back, and night after night, when the house was closed, she would sit listening for the footstep that she believed one day she should hear again. She is still living. A little while ago I had a letter from her son. "The mystery of my father's fate," he wrote, "is still unsolved."

It is impossible to conclude that this unfortunate man meant to disappear. He would have cashed the cheque had flight been in his mind. Men who intend to live anywhere must have money. The cheque was never presented. For his own personal use he had for weeks previously drawn nothing out of the bank.

What became of him? Was he lured down some byway and murdered for his watch and chain and whatever he had in his pocket, and his body disposed of in the mysterious way that murdered people are got rid of even to this day? Or was it a case of dual identity? Did he, forgetting who he was, think himself some one else, and live and work as some one else in some other part of England until he died in the natural course of events?

That *may* happen, and does sometimes account for mysterious disappearances.

A man well-known in the theatrical profession some years ago—the touring manager of a popular London lessee—once disappeared mysteriously. His accounts were in order. He had paid the company and remitted the balance to his chief. And having done so he disappeared. The company waited for him at a railway station, and waited in vain. All sorts of conjectures were indulged in, and his friends and relatives were untiring in their efforts to ascertain his fate.

Late one night an actor going home to his residence on the south side of the water turned up a side street, attracted by a little crowd in it. A gang of roughs were around two men who were fighting.

The actor stopped for a moment to "study character," and then went on up the side street, knowing that at the top of it he would get into the main thoroughfare again.

Near the top he came to a public-house. Outside the house a poorly-clad street musician was playing a cornet—none too well—and collecting coppers from the people in the bar. The actor looked at the comet-player for a moment, and then, with a cry of astonishment, touched him on the shoulder and called him by name.

It was the touring manager whose mysterious disappearance had been the talk of the profession.

The poor fellow was absolutely ignorant of his own identity. It was some time afterwards before old familiar surroundings and the voices and faces of old friends revived in his brain the memory of the past and gave him back his lost identity.

It happens sometimes that the mystery of a disappearance is penetrated only to increase the anguish of the unhappy relatives. A young man of good family, becoming heavily involved through gambling transactions, left his home. The efforts of his father to ascertain his whereabouts were fruitless.

Many years afterwards the young man's father, Mr. ———, was at the house of a friend who collected souvenirs of famous crimes. In his collection was an album containing the portraits of murderers and their victims.

Turning over the pages of the album, Mr. ——— uttered an exclamation of terror. "Who is that?" he exclaimed, pointing to the portrait of a young man in the uniform of a private soldier.

"That," said the friend, "was a soldier who shot his sergeant dead in the barrack-yard. He was tried, and it was proved at the trial that he had shown symptoms of insanity before committing the act. He was sent to Broadmoor."

The unhappy father went to the great criminal lunatic asylum, and there found his son a hopeless maniac. He had enlisted under a false name, and under that name had been tried. The father read the case in the papers at the time, but had no idea it was his own son who was being tried for his life.

The secret of many a mysterious disappearance lies buried in the earth, sometimes in cellars, behind brick walls, beneath the flooring of a kitchen or an outhouse, in the garden, in the farmyard. We even know that people who have disappeared mysteriously out of life may be lying securely packed and stored away in a great furniture repository.

Miss Hacker had lain in the coal-cellar that was her grave for two years before chance brought her body to light. Miss Holland might be lying now in the Moat Farm had not Dougal gone to the Bank of England to cash certain notes, the numbers of which had been forwarded to the bank authorities.

When the house of a fashionable physician in the West End of London was being re-drained some years ago, the body of a beautiful girl was discovered buried under the flooring. There was no clue to her identity, and the coroner's verdict was given on the body of "some person unknown."

But there are other ways of disposing of the bodies of people whose mysterious disappearance is due to an act of violence.

William Smith has disappeared. He leaves home in the ordinary way and never returns. There is nothing to account for his disappearance. He was in no difficulty. He was happy in his domestic circumstances. He has taken no money away with him, apparently. Every search is made for him, but no trace of him, living or dead, can be found.

But he has been murdered and buried—buried in a cemetery with the rites of the church, and there is a tombstone above his grave—only somebody else's name is on it.

This is what happened.

A certain person owed him a sum of money, or he was threatening proceedings against a certain person, or for some reason—as in the famous Northumberland Street tragedy—it was to the interest of a certain person to get him into a house and murder him.

The trap was laid. William Smith met his enemy—the enemy invited him to his house, his chambers, or his flat. A sudden blow felled the victim to the ground and killed him.

How could the body be disposed of? The clerk to a Burial Board who gave evidence before the Committee of the House of Commons explains the whole process.

To show that I am not imagining or exaggerating I will give the exact words from the report "ordered by the House of Commons to be printed 15th August and 1st September, 1893." The evidence is given on page 19 of the

Select Committee's Report. "You do not want a certificate to bury a body; you can dispose of a body in the London Cemetery without any certificate at all. If any gentleman here was murdered, to put it plainly, and you had a queer undertaker to dispose of that body, he could dispose of it without any one being any the wiser."

"2343. How could he dispose of it?—I will give you an instance. Say I am an undertaker, and I have got the body of a man named William Smith to be buried to-morrow at Finchley, and he is registered all right. A person comes to me at eleven o'clock at night and says, 'I have got a body to get rid of, and I will give you £500 to do it.' The undertaker takes the body he has got to get rid of to Finchley, and buries it as William Smith without a certificate; we send that notice to the registrar, who refers to his book, and finds that it is quite right. Then the undertaker will take the real William Smith to Ilford Cemetery, say, and take the body up there with a certificate, which saves any inquiry being made.

"2344. What does he do with the other body?—He has already taken that up without a certificate to Finchley Cemetery; he buries the body he has got to get rid of at Finchley, and withholds the certificate of William Smith; the authorities then give notice to the registrar that William Smith was buried there, and the certificate was not delivered. The undertaker has that certificate in his possession then, and he can take the original William Smith up to another cemetery, and there they do not trouble, because they get a certificate delivered with the body.

"2345. In that way you think it is very easy to get rid of a body if any one desires to do so?—Yes, unless there was a law passed that no body should be interred without a burial certificate being delivered at the time."

That is the manner in which a murdered body might be disposed of. The friends and relatives would be in complete ignorance of the fate of the man who had disappeared. It would remain for ever a mystery.

No wonder the Committee of the House of Commons embodied this paragraph in their report: "It is a most important duty of society to guard its members against foul play, and it appears to your Committee that so far as may be it should be made impossible for any person to disappear from his place in the community without any satisfactory evidence being obtained of the cause of his disappearance."

All the people who disappear and are never heard of again do not start fresh lives. Many of them are without the means to do so. Some have probably committed suicide. All the people who quietly drop into the Thames do not come to the surface again. Something may happen to prevent the body rising. But for a suicide to remain long a mystery is the exception, not the rule. The suicide does not go out of the way to take precautions against the discovery of the deed. The average person bent on suicide more frequently desires the sympathy which will follow the discovery of the tragedy.

As a matter of fact, romance and crime divide the mysterious disappearances fairly between them, and if there is a balance either way it is in favour of crime.

The person who remains alive after disappearing has a task of the greatest difficulty in these days of photography and illustrated journalism. The odds against being able to avoid discovery are enormous. It is only the dead and buried who are safely out of the way of prying eyes.

And yet there are cases on record of people who have disappeared and been completely lost to their relatives who have never moved five miles away from their home.

James Ferguson, the famous astronomer, was walking one day in the Strand with his daughter. They stopped together to look in a shop window. When Mr. Ferguson moved on to renew his walk, his daughter was nowhere to be seen.

Her fate was a mystery which was only solved long years afterwards when she was discovered dying in a room in a court not many yards from the spot at which she had disappeared.

She had slipped away from her father to meet a lover, and with him she had eloped. He deserted her, and the unhappy girl, after trying to be an actress, and trying to be an authoress, sank to the lowest level, and for three years before she was found dying she had haunted the Strand and had often at night encountered friends and relatives who had not recognized her.

Some years ago, in Bermondsey Workhouse, two old paupers who had been fellow-inmates of the house for fifteen years fell into conversation over their afternoon pipes.

They became reminiscent. "Ah!" said one, "my mother lived in that street"—alluding to one that was then being pulled down. "She was a widow, and I and my brother helped in the shop. One day my brother disappeared. He was seventeen. He went out and we never saw him again—never knew what happened to him."

"He helped your mother in a shop in that street," said the other pauper. "What sort of a shop?"

"A greengrocer's—it was the little shop at the corner."

"What was your brother's name?"

"William Jones."

The other pauper rose and held out his hand.

"Tom!" he exclaimed, "it's wonderful! Here have we two brothers been in this workhouse together for fifteen years and we didn't know each other!"

Then the man told his story. He had got into a bit of trouble about some money with another young man in the neighbourhood, and had been worried about it. So he had said nothing to his mother, but gone away and got a job in another part of London. There he had married and settled down, brought up a family, lost his wife, lost his children, fallen on evil days, and at last became a pauper.

For fifteen years the man who had mysteriously disappeared had been under the same roof as his brother, and neither had known the other.

CHAPTER XIII
THE FAMILY SKELETON

The old-fashioned housekeeper—A ghost which fought the servant— Jealously guarding the family secret—An adventure while primrose gathering—A silent dinner-party— Dwarfs who live with the children

IN the days of romance the Secret Chamber was part of every mansion that had any claim to antiquity. Every old castle, every nobleman's seat, had in it a room which could be used on an emergency for the stowing away of something or somebody that it was not considered advisable for the visitors or the retainers to see.

Many of these secret chambers still exist, and the families to whom they belong are rather proud of them. The housekeeper who takes you over an ancient seat will conduct you to a room at the end of a passage—sometimes you can approach it through a sliding panel—and tell you in parrot fashion the tragedy connected with it. Occasionally there is a ghost attached to the story, and the housekeeper assures you that many members of the family have seen it.

The gruesomeness of the room in which a murder was committed three hundred years ago is heightened when your guide points to a stain on the floor and tells you that all the processes of modern scrubbing and cleaning have failed to remove it.

There is a house in the North of England which has a secret room, the exact position of which is only revealed to two people—the heir-at-law and the family solicitor. Hundreds of visitors have tried in vain to find it.

There is a country house which has a secret room in which there lives an old lady—a very ghostly old lady, for she died and was buried a hundred years ago. Only on rare occasions does she appear to the other occupants, and then she is attired in an old-fashioned brown dress, with a lace cap on her head and a bunch of keys in her hand.

My friend and collaborator, the late Frederic Clay, went to stay at this house. He knew nothing of the story. After he had been shown to his room to dress for dinner an old lady, attired in brown, and carrying a bunch of keys in her hand, came in.

He thought she was the housekeeper, and said he was quite comfortable and wanted nothing. Then she went away.

At dinner he said to his hostess—a relative: "What a dear old lady your housekeeper is! But what an old-fashioned way she dresses!—she looks as if she had stepped out of an old romance."

There was dead silence at the table. The next morning he learned that the old lady of the secret room had paid him a visit.

That was a modern instance; but most of the stories and tales of old romance are associated with family traditions, and the mystery of them belongs to a day that is long since dead.

But here in the heart of London, in the midst of the traffic of the crowded capital, even where the omnibuses pass the door, there are secret chambers and uncanny sights hidden away from prying eyes.

As a rule the old retainers, the servants who have been with the family for years, share the knowledge; but it is carefully guarded from new-corners.

Not long ago a young servant came to seek a place in London. She had been housemaid at a rectory, and the rector's wife gave her an excellent character. She went to a West End agency, and after a few days she was engaged as third housemaid by a dear, white-headed old lady, who said she was the housekeeper to Lord and Lady ————. The girl went to her situation. The house was in an aristocratic square, and the girl, from what she saw of her surroundings, thought she was fortunate in getting the place.

She had to share a bedroom with another servant, a middle-aged woman, who had been with the family for many years.

In the middle of the night the country girl was aroused by a strange sound. She started up. The moonlight streaming in through the window fell upon a tall, gaunt woman with dishevelled hair, who was standing at the foot of the bed.

The girl uttered a cry, and the servant sleeping in the same room woke up and sprang out of bed. She seized the "apparition" by the arms and held her. In a moment another woman, partially dressed, entered the room, and the two dragged the "apparition," fighting and screaming, out into the passage.

When her fellow-servant returned, the girl, who was paralyzed with fear, asked her what had happened.

"Nothing," was the reply. "I thought I heard one of the girls in the other room calling out, and I went to see if she was ill."

"But I saw a woman—a woman standing here—here by the bed," gasped the terrified girl. "I saw you help to drag her out of the room."

"Nonsense, my dear; you've been dreaming. That's nightmare. Go to sleep and don't talk such foolishness."

The girl lay awake all night. In the morning she went to the housekeeper and said that she must go. She couldn't stop another night in the place after what she had seen.

The housekeeper heard her story and told her she was fancying things—there was nobody of that sort in the house. But, of course, if the girl wanted to go she could.

The girl left, and went to the agency to explain matters, and to ask them to get her another situation.

The manageress of the agency listened to her story and said nothing. But she remembered that two years previously a servant on their books had left through seeing something of the same sort. On that occasion the girl had described it as a ghost.

The truth of the matter was this. The apparition was that of a mad woman—the daughter of the house, a woman of five-and-thirty. Her father and mother had engaged a female keeper, and kept the poor demented creature at home. Ordinarily she was quiet enough. But at times she became cunning or violent, and, escaping from the apartment at the top of the house in which she was kept, made her way into a room occupied by others.

The family entertained and had frequent visitors, but only the most intimate of their relatives knew that in the upper part of the house there was a mad woman under restraint.

There is a fine house standing in its own grounds in the northern part of London. It is occupied by a wealthy family, and none of the large staff of servants are presumably aware of the secret that the family jealously guard.

All they know is that the upper part of one wing of the house, which they never enter, is occupied by their mistress's father, an old gentleman, who is bedridden, and is rather eccentric and dislikes strange faces. For this reason he has his own valet and an aged man-servant to attend to him, and these are the only people, with the exception of the master and mistress, who ever go into that part of the house.

But the mistress's bedridden father is a fiction. The rooms in reality are occupied by the son of the house—a son whom, owing to his terrible disfigurement, it would have been more merciful to have strangled at his birth, but who has been loved and reared and tended to live apart from his fellow-men.

The unhappy young man's sisters have never seen him. It would not be right that they should be allowed to look upon a terrible affliction which, in common parlance, is called "a freak of nature." Only the father and mother, the two attendants, and the family doctor know how terrible the affliction is, or how shocking is the tragedy the unhappy parents are guarding in the "secret chambers" of their home.

All the "freaks," all the strange deformities, are not the offspring of poor parents, who permit them to be seen or exhibited. The joined twins, the sideshow phenomena of nature, are born in all ranks of society.

Only now and again does the world know of the tragedy—for tragedy it is—in the family circle of the well-to-do.

The "misfortune" is concealed. Every precaution is taken against publicity.

Sometimes the "afflicted" member of the family is sent away to be guarded and cared for in a medically-superintended home specially arranged for the reception of such "patients."

There is a London doctor who has a home of this sort. If you were conducted over it, and saw its inmates, you would think that he must have nerves of iron to pass his life in such weird companionship. Young, middle-aged, and old, the patients are every one of them so marred by nature that ordinary life among their fellow-creatures is impossible.

Once in my life, trespassing in a private wood in search of primroses, I came suddenly upon a group of human beings so strange in their appearance, so awful, that for a moment I believed that I was the victim of an hallucination.

It was only when a gentleman came hurriedly up to me, demanding to know what I wanted, and I had explained that I had only trespassed in search of wild flowers, that I learnt the wood formed part of the grounds of a private asylum in which the "afflicted" members of wealthy families were received. I understood then what the terrible scene I had witnessed meant, and I hastened to apologize for my unintentional intrusion.

But a mother's love is not for beauty of form or soundness of mind, and so it frequently happens that the suffering one is dearer to her than all, and is never allowed to be taken from her fostering care.

Still, she cannot expect that it will be looked on by strangers—not always by its own kith and kin—with the eyes of love through which she sees it, and so there is a portion of the dwelling-place set apart—a room, or rooms, where no one but herself and one trusted attendant ever enters.

There the sufferer lives, cut off from the world—a prisoner, in a sense—and passes from childhood to youth, sometimes from youth to middle-age, its very existence unknown to the friends who from time to time visit the house and join the family circle.

Because the secret is so carefully guarded, this phase of our poor humanity is unfamiliar to us. Its existence is hardly suspected. But it is the lifelong sorrow in many a home that the world thinks a happy one.

When the sorrow is that of a noble family, and the afflicted one is the heir to a proud name and a vast estate, we hear of it. The secret cannot in such circumstances always be guarded. A whisper of it is certain to get about. But with those less conspicuously before the world the secret may be kept until the grave hides it for ever.

Into the more painful—I will not say repulsive—phase of this subject I do not desire to enter; it is right that that which shocks and horrifies should be kept from the public gaze.

But on certain phases which are sad and pathetic, without being repulsive, it may be permissible to dwell for a moment.

From his vast establishment in the City a prosperous merchant returns nightly to his beautiful home in the environs of London. He is a widower with four grown-up daughters. He receives no company. Every evening he dines alone with his daughters. All four are deaf mutes, and the dinner-party is one of unbroken silence. He has never heard the sound of his children's voices. They have never heard a word that fell from his lips. He does not talk of his trouble. Few people, except his near relatives, know of it. It is a family secret carefully guarded. These deaf mutes are women, the youngest is five-and-twenty. They will never marry. To the end of his days the prosperous city merchant will live his family life with the four daughters, who can neither hear nor speak.

As I write I think of another home I know, in which the father and mother have three children to keep them company, to listen to them, to talk with them, to share in the family joys and sorrows. But these children, though they have not been separated for a single day, have never seen each other. They are all blind.

There is a gentle lady with silvered hair, renowned for her charity and the good use she has made of the wealth her husband left her. You will see her wherever she goes accompanied by her two daughters. There is a third, who is the eldest. But the eldest daughter is never seen. Even those who are privileged visitors to the house are not aware of her existence. She is five-and-thirty. But when there are no visitors, and she comes and sits with her mother and sisters, this woman of five-and-thirty behaves like a child of seven. She nurses a doll. She is fitful and wayward as a child, and has naughty childish ways. She is spoken to as a child, caressed as a child, reproved as a child.

Hers is a strange and peculiar case. Her mental development ceased when she attained the age of seven. Her body became that of a woman, her brain remained that of a child. She reads books intended for the nursery. She cries like a child at a trivial ill. I have seen few sights more pathetic than this woman of five-and-thirty, her dark hair prematurely streaked with grey, nursing her doll and reading the stories in the child's picture-book that is sometimes given to her to keep her quiet.

Every Sunday as I walk to the West there passes me a school of crippled children. In the ranks of the cripples there walk always four dwarfs—four little old women well past middle-age. They are shorter than the shortest little girls in the school. They are so small that children of seven and eight tower above them.

These old ladies hold hands and walk like the little ones. But one of them is over sixty, and they have passed the greater part of their lives in the institution which exists for little crippled girls.

These old ladies have left their homes to be tended here among the children. With the littles ones they do not attract much attention. It is only when you look at them closely you see that they are not children themselves.

The dwarfs who are born in well-to-do families are not put away; they remain part of the family circle. But because of their presence in it, there is frequently restraint in the matter of acquaintanceship. The dwarf, always intelligent, frequently gentle and affectionate, is loved as dearly as any of the healthy children who thrive and grow. But that it may be spared pain and the pitying glance the home is not as other homes. The "secret," if not guarded, is not obtruded. There is one member of the family who is not seen by the ordinary visitor, who does not take his or her meals at the table when visitors are under the roof.

Even in humbler homes there are sometimes mysteries. There are those who are loved and cared for who never leave the house in the daytime, but see what little of the world may be permitted them after nightfall.

You may sometimes see a woman so closely veiled that her features are indistinguishable being led along the Embankment by the river in the dusk of a summer's evening. The story of that veiled woman is a heartrending one. She was a beautiful girl and about to be married to the man she loved when a woman mad with jealousy flung vitriol in her face. Her life was saved, but it would have been almost better had she died. From that hour only her mother has looked upon her face. From the rest of the world it is mercifully veiled.

Sometimes the secret chamber hides not a misfortune, but a crime. There is an insanity of criminality which delights in the torture of the weak, the suffering, the mentally deficient. Now and again the world is startled by the narrative of secret cruelty practised on helpless children, of an afflicted wife kept as a prisoner neglected and ill-treated. There have been cases in which the presence in a house of one of these victims of monstrous cruelty has remained unsuspected for years. The secret of the "prisoner" has only been revealed by an accident.

Not long ago the mystery of a secret chamber in a humble house in a poor street in Hoxton was discovered.

The school-board officer goes to every house and enters every home in order to see that the children are attending school.

In this home there was no child ever to be discovered. But the officer had information that a little girl of eight was undoubtedly a member of the family.

One night, "in consequence of information received," as the police say, he kept watch, and at nine o'clock he saw the mother come out of the house cautiously, look around, and then return to emerge with a little girl. The officer, who had taken precautions against recognition, followed, and then the mystery was solved.

The little girl was earning the living of her parents by performing at a variety theatre. To prevent the interference of the school authorities the parents kept her shut up all day in the bedroom, and only brought her oat of It to take her to the music-hall.

There are secret chambers in London houses still, the mystery of which has yet to be revealed; some which may remain undiscovered, to be "mysteries" in the daily press fifty or a hundred years hence. The bricked-up cellar that thrills us in the pages of Edgar Allan Poe is playing its part in the criminal tragedies of the twentieth-century Babylon.

CHAPTER XIV
THE ROMANCE OF POVERTY

Noblemen who live in mean streets—A peer on a pound a week—A princess out in service—Lodgekeeper where once mistress—A grave-digger with royal blood—From £100,000 to nothing

Poverty has so many romances, and they are so varied.

Under the humblest roofs in this great city of ours men and women are daily writing in the book of life beautiful stories of tender love, of noble self-sacrifice, of deeds of heroic endurance. There are idylls of the slums and alleys as charming as ever poet penned; there are stories to be told of the dwellers in mean streets that lift our thoughts far above the sordid things of earth.

But these are romances pure and simple, and in them is no element of mystery. The romances I have in my mind as I write are those in which the poverty conceals from the eyes of the world a truth it would be greatly interested to learn.

When the London season is at its height the daily papers are filled with the gay or great doings of the aristocracy. Every movement is chronicled as being of surpassing interest to the general public. If my lord and my lady entertain their friends at home the details are considered as important as those of a battle in the Far East or a debate in the House of Commons. Even if my lord or my lady dine or sup at a restaurant the fact is duly chronicled. The untitled leaders of the smart set, our wealthy American visitors, the stars of the opera and the stage, share in the general publicity. Celebrities, whether of rank or wealth or talent, are standing items of "Fashionable Intelligence." All the world is made familiar with their features, and their diaries are compiled for them by the staff, male and female, of the popular periodicals.

There are men and women of noble birth and ancient lineage, there are men and women who have been famous in their day in the world of fashion and of art, over whose lives a great silence has settled, who move about in our midst, their very identity unsuspected, who know sorrow and suffering, and sometimes even privation. These are the romances of poverty which are mysteries, because they are rarely fathomed. Now and again the veil is lifted in the hospital, in the parish infirmary, or at the coroner's inquest. But many of them remain hidden for ever by the shallow earth which covers a pauper's coffin.

There is an old, grey-headed gentleman in thread-bare, shiny clothes, who comes out of his poor lodgings in a mean street daily when it is fine and sits in the park. He brings with him a rusty brown bag that once was black. From that bag he takes soon after midday a little packet containing a slice or two of bread and a small piece of cheese. When he has finished his humble meal he walks to the public drinking-fountain and takes a cup of water.

If the society reporter wished to chronicle this midday meal in the "Fashionable Intelligence," this is how he would have to word his paragraph in order to be correct: "Among the company who lunched in Regent's Park to-day was Lord ─────────. His lordship is at present occupying one room in Great James Street, Lisson Grove, where he is staying incognito under the name of Mr. Wilson."

The old gentleman, who is so poor that he can only afford bread and cheese for lunch—it is his dinner—and one room in Lisson Grove, bears a name as noble as any in the pages of Burke. His ancestral home is one of the show-places of England. But it passed from his family nearly a hundred years ago, when the reverse of fortune came that left a noble house beggared.

Lord ───────── is quite alone now. Her ladyship died a year or two ago. She added to the poor little income by shirt-making at home for a West End firm.

When her ladyship died his lordship had an income of 10s. a week. This was generously increased to £1 by a relative who was just a little better off. On £1 a week one of England's "old nobility" is passing a peaceful old age. He has always a smile for the little children who play near him in the park. Sometimes when they see him bring out his bread they think he is going to feed the ducks. But he cannot afford to do that.

Ducks want such big pieces. But now and then he spares a few crumbs for the sparrows.

The parish doctor stood by the bedside of a woman who had been brought to the infirmary some days previously from a common lodging-house in the neighbourhood.

The woman was dying, but quite conscious. The workhouse-master was with the doctor.

"It's an extraordinary story she tells," said the master. "She says she is the Marchioness of ─────────."

The doctor looked pityingly at the poor creature, who was in the last stage of a fatal disease, and bent down to listen to something she was saying.

"It's quite true," she said. "We separated, you know, a good many years ago, and I never saw him afterwards. What was the good? But I should like him to know I'm dying—if you can find him."

The doctor, hearing the name of the nobleman, remembered something of the story. He went away and made inquiries, which resulted in his being able to find the dying woman's husband.

The Marquis, an elderly man, came to the bedside of his dying wife and forgave her. He waited till the end. When the Marchioness was dead he shook hands with the doctor, thanked him for his kindness, and said he would try and get enough money to have her ladyship decently buried. He kept his word.

Five years afterwards the doctor was rung up at one o'clock in the morning. He put his head out of the window and found that the Marquis had called upon him.

"Doctor," said the Marquis, "I'm married again, and I want you to come to my wife at once."

In the early hours of the morning an heir to the ancient title was born in lodgings in a little suburban side street.

Up to the present the doctor has not received his fee. He did not press for it. He knew how terribly straitened were the circumstances of the nobleman, whose first wife died in the work-house, and whose second wife presented him with an heir in cheap London lodgings.

In a recent book on Russian life it is told how a young woman who had applied for the position of lady's-maid hesitated to produce her papers of identification when asked by the lady who wished to engage her. "Ah! Madame," the girl sobbed, "when you see who I am you will not take me as your servant, and I have been so long looking for a home and work by which I may live."

The lady, expecting some dreadful revelation, was astonished, when the "papers" were reluctantly handed to her, to find that the applicant for a situation as a domestic servant was of noble birth—a princess, in fact.

Princesses do not go into service in England. But ladies of title, concealing their identity, sometimes try to find a home and employment by becoming servants.

There came to me some years ago a middle-aged lady of refined and gentle appearance. She had heard that I wanted a cook, and she pleaded to be allowed to take the situation.

I told her frankly that I did not think she was a cook in the domestic sense of the word, and I asked her where she had been employed. Eventually the poor lady confided in me.

The story she told was a simple one and a very old one. The solicitor who, after her husband's death, had the management of her affairs had absconded, and she and her daughter found themselves penniless. The daughter, having a good voice and appearance, obtained an engagement in the chorus of a travelling opera company. The mother, dropping her title and changing her name, went to a registry office and entered herself on the books as a cook. In her youth she had had a taste for cooking, and had been one of the first to take lessons when it became the fashion for ladies to master the details of the culinary art.

Lady ———— had some trouble about references, but, confiding in an old friend who knew of her qualifications, she got over the difficulty. In her first situation she was uncomfortable, and after three months she left. But, fortified with a reference, she obtained a situation in a good family. There it more than once happened that Lady ———— cooked for people who had been guests at her own table in her husband's lifetime. They would have been considerably astonished had they known that their former hostess was acting in the capacity of paid cook in the kitchen of the house in which they were dining. A break-down in health compelled Lady ———— to give up her situation. It was after her recovery—the little she had been able to save by hard work swallowed up in the expenses of her illness—that she came to me, hoping I might put her in the way of getting some articles she had written on "Cooking for Ladies" accepted by a newspaper. When I last heard of Lady ———— she was going out to cook on what I believe is called "the job."

Here is a little tobacconist's shop in the suburbs. The customers who enter it daily for their cigars and tobacco, sometimes for a box of lights, and see a neatly dressed lady, who is the proprietress, behind the counter, have not the slightest idea that the lady who supplies them with their packets of cigarettes and ounces of tobacco has a "handle to her name," that her husband is the heir to an earldom, and that in due course the fair tobacconist who is keeping a little shop for a livelihood will have a right to, sit among the peeresses of England as the Countess of ————.

In the environs of London there is a comely old lady who lives in the lodge on a great estate. Sometimes she comes out and opens the park gate that the occupants of a magnificent carriage may drive up to the Hall, which is their residence. The residents at the Hall are wealthy Americans. The old lady is the widow of the former owner. It was the home of his ancestors for three centuries. To the Hall he brought her as a bride to be its mistress. Now she is the lodge-keeper. Her husband before he died was employed as a coachman to a-wealthy City merchant. It was this merchant who recommended the widow to the Americans as a trustworthy woman to have the lodge.

Even the descendants of kings come upon evil times and bring the Crown of England into the romance of poverty. The sexton of a West End church was one of the co-heirs to the barony in a famous peerage claim concerning which evidence was given before the House of Lords. This gentleman, who followed the humble occupation of a grave-digger, was entitled to quarter the Royal Arms. His direct descent from Thomas Plantagenet, Duke of Gloucester, fifth son of Edward III, was undisputed. A barefooted, ragged little lad playing in a back court in Wapping is the descendant of the O'Neills, the scion of a race of kings renowned in Irish history.

In one of the worst streets of London, a street that is painted in the blackest colours in Mr. Charles Booth's great and exhaustive work, there is a house let out in rooms. The inhabitants of this street are mostly criminals. They are frankly classified as thieves, burglars, and bullies. But in this house, if we enter it, we shall find a man of education and refinement occupying with his wife and child two humble, scantily furnished rooms. If you know the neighbourhood, the "appearance" of this family at once rivets your attention. Their features, their neatness and cleanliness, their speech—all are in direct contrast to anything you have met with in the locality.

In what circumstances they have drifted to such a neighbourhood as this I do not know; but their poverty they confess themselves. The man is in bad health. He is waiting till he gets a little stronger to find something to do. In the meantime he is living in a neighbourhood in which it is not safe for a decent person to be abroad after nightfall. He has been knocked down twice himself. His respectable appearance led the inhabitants of the street to imagine that he must have some money about him.

This man bears an honoured name. Living where he does, there is no need for him to conceal it. To the thieves and hooligans who are his neighbours the name means nothing. Respectable people never come down the street. Knowing his name, his ancestry, and the position his kith and kin have held in public life, the man is to me a mystery. His poverty I can understand—I have seen the brother of a world-famous divine in a wretched room in a slum in the Borough, and I have seen his children given boots that they should not have to go barefooted to school in the winter-time—but this man has hidden himself away in a criminal area, in a street that is notorious, and here with his wife and child he must rub shoulders night and day with the vilest of the vile.

To live by choice in a street where you are liable to be brutally assaulted directly you put your nose outside your door is an act the motive of which is difficult to fathom.

A little way out of London, on the road to a popular Thames-side resort, there is a tavern with a tea-garden attached to it. All day long on Sunday traps pull up there, and the occupants get out and refresh while the ostlers water the horses.

Sometimes the ladies of the party remain in the trap and take their refreshment there. To them there comes with shuffling feet an old, grey-headed waiter, who is specially engaged to do the "outside Sunday work." He takes the order and returns with the required "refreshment" on a tray. When he is paid, and receives a penny or twopence for himself, the old fellow returns thanks and doffs his weather-beaten cap to the ladies in quite the old-world courtly style.

There was a time in the days long ago when he raised a glossy high hat in the same courtly way—not to the ladies in a one-horse wagonette or a pony-trap, but to the ladies in smart victorias and aristocratic barouches. And he drove his own horses, too—a splendid pair that made many a lounger in the park look after his mail phaeton and admire his "cattle."

He could have signed his name to a cheque for £100,000 in those days, and the cheque would have been paid by his bankers.

He had not made his money. It had been made for him by his father, a man of renown in the City, the head of a firm that had been honourably known in commerce for many generations.

His father, with an ample fortune, retired from the business and left that fortune to his son, who had nothing to do but live as a private gentleman.

He lived that life till he was forty. Then a large portion of his capital was lost by an unwise investment, and from that day things began to go badly, and in a few years he found himself penniless. His wife, who had been accustomed to every comfort and luxury, died before the final disaster came, and left him with a daughter who was a cripple and an invalid.

Father and daughter faced adversity bravely. Together they managed to, pay the rent of a small cottage at Chiswick. The daughter was clever with her needle and did fancy work at home; the father obtained a situation as waiter, and was sent out with provision vans to children's treats and picnics. But he got too old for that, and at last was glad of the Sunday job on which we have seen him engaged.

The man who could once sign his cheque for £100,000 is grateful for the pennies that he gets from the "pull-up" parties. When the Sunday is fine he goes back to his invalid daughter with a smiling face. When the Sunday is wet he goes home with a smile all the same—but his heart is as heavy as his pocket is light.

There died recently under tragic circumstances a man whom I had seen rise to heights he had never dreamed of in his youth. Handsome, agreeable, and refined, everybody liked him and said he would do well. But from a humble beginning he rose to honours and dignities. He held an official position that gave him a magnificent equipage to ride in, and the honour conferred upon him made his wife "her ladyship."

He gave grand entertainments and receptions, and his name was constantly before the world in the public prints. His daughter attended a fashionable school and was fetched every day by a footman.

I saw him in his splendour, and complimented him on the favours that Fortune had showered upon him with such a lavish hand.

Years went by, and gradually his name disappeared from the public journals. He dropped out. The world moved on, and nobody troubled very much what had become of him.

Then one day I saw him again. He passed me in the street.

The man I had seen honoured, féted, and acclaimed had come to the point at which he shunned his friends. I would have stopped and spoken, but he hurried past me.

Three weeks later I heard of his death. He had died penniless. He had known the torture of penury for years.

And "her ladyship," broken-hearted, tortured by the memory of the past magnificence, had eaten her heart out in sorrow by the side of the man she loved.

I had seen their gorgeous carriage pass with its mounted escort through acclaiming crowds. Husband and wife died tragically. The daughter who used to be fetched from school by the family footman died not long ago of starvation in circumstances of the most intense pathos.

About this romance of poverty there was, alas! the grim note of a poignant realism. But it was a mystery that only the tragedy of its victims' deaths revealed.

CHAPTER XV
THE GARDEN OF GUILT

Slums in the gilded West—"It's the place! It's ruin to us all"—Where the children earn and the mothers drink—How the "till sneak" works—Lynch law in London—A slump depression in the burglary trade

IN all great cities there are certain areas which bear an evil reputation. On the principle that birds of a feather dock together, the vicious and the criminal have a habit of seeking each other's society. But though crime and vice are frequently associated, there is often a sharp distinction to be drawn so far as certain quarters of London are concerned.

In the heart of the West End, in the Royal Borough of Kensington itself, there are whole streets in which the inhabitants are vicious, as we understand the word as a label. Here the police are busy, but the bulk of the charges brought against the women and the men are for drunkenness, for disorderly conduct, for fighting and brawling. They are principally night charges, for during the day you may wander the neighbourhood and see little life in the streets that are notoriously ill-famed.

There is one street that from end to end has not a single house in it where there is not a broken window. These houses are packed with a low type of humanity. Every house is a lodging-house, and many of them are lodging-houses for women only.

In the daytime drunken, dissipated-looking women loll in the doorways or thrust their tousled heads out of the upper windows. If you enter these houses and go down into the common kitchen you will find scores of women, young and middle-aged, sitting round the coke fires, listless, often morose. Among them you will see now and again women with traces of refinement, some whose features still bear the lingering traces of youth and good looks.

But they are lost souls every one of them. There is not one among the hundreds who crowd the notorious lodging-houses of this terrible guilt garden of the West who is still making an effort to earn an honest livelihood. Most of them are thieves when opportunity offers. They are not professional thieves, but many of them are in league with rascals of the worst type, loafers and hooligans, who are not ashamed to beat and maltreat women and force money from them.

This district is a district of despair to the philanthropist, the social reformer, and the Christian worker. It has been called the Avenue of the West. It is a cesspool to which all that is worst in the squalid vice of the capital flows. And the pity of it is that the stream is constantly fed by tributaries from the cleaner, greener land beyond. It is here that hundreds of our rural immigrants drift in ignorance or in despair of London's vastness and inhospitality, and here they rapidly deteriorate, and become in time as evil as their environment.

There is no mystery about the character of the people in these streets of shame. And yet the element of mystery greets you at every turn, whether you wander these byways of wickedness by day or by night.

If you would explore the mysteries of the Avernus, it is not in the houses or the streets that you will see the veil lifted.

But stand with me in this room in the school where the mentally and physically feeble offspring of degenerate parents are cared for and taught. Listen to the cry of a woman, who pours her heart out to the sympathetic teacher who has sent for her to give her advice about her little boy.

"It's the place, miss," wails the woman. "It's ruin to us all to be in it. It's ruined his father—it's ruined me, and it's ruining the children. If I could only get out of it! But I can't—I never shall now."

Ten years ago this woman and her husband came from the country to try their luck in London. The man failed to get work, fell in with evil companions, and they drifted to the Avernus. The husband is a loafer—the wife does a little work at a laundry when she can get it. They live in a vile street, where oaths and foul language and brutal deeds are all they hear and see. The house they live in is filled with bad characters. The eldest boy—he came a bright-eyed, rosy-cheeked child from the country with his parents—is in prison; the girl, who was born after they came to the Avernus, is in an idiot asylum; the boy at the school is developing criminal tendencies. The mother sees with despair the ruin of her family, but she is helpless to avert it. Her husband is a drunkard. She herself has fallen into the slough at last.

Her case is typical of hundreds in the neighbourhood. So terrible is the effect of the environment on the children that day and night the Industrial School officers are searching for girls and boys, whose only hope of salvation is to be separated from their parents.

If you were to spend one night in the Avernus your face would be crimson with righteous indignation that little children should live open-eared and open-eyed in constant contact with such horrors.

Do you see a broad-shouldered, burly, kindly-looking man walking quietly along the street? As he comes into sight a group of lads and lasses disperse as if by magic. There is a sudden bolt up a narrow passage that through a back street leads into the open thoroughfare.

The big man smiles good-humouredly. He has seen the group, and the girl he wants was in it. He will find her before the night is over, because he will enter every house she is likely to have taken refuge in. He is the Industrial School's officer. Three years ago he rescued a girl from evil surroundings and she was sent to Canada. She has managed in some mysterious way to get back again across the sea, and has headed straight for the Avernus, where she has a bad mother, and a father who is worse.

There is nothing brings the shame and degradation of one phase of London life so acutely home to you as a day and a night with the officers whose duty it is to remove the young from the homes and haunts of vice. In one street in the Avernus there are two hundred children growing up. There is not one house in the whole of that street that does not harbour women of the most degraded type.

Many of these children are already busy as money-makers. Some of them are sent out into the streets to beg; to play their carefully planned tricks and dodges on the humanity of the passers-by. There are women who wash their faces, smooth their hair, and dress in seedy black as widows, and take little children out with them to beg. These "poor widows" starve the children and spend the money in drink. Sometimes they don't take their own children; they hire a deformed child or a cripple of a mother who is willing to let it out. There are hundreds of little children now in industrial homes who were forced into the streets to ply the trade of mendicity and mendacity, and who were treated with the most brutal violence by their parents if they came home empty-handed. Many a child, failing to get money by begging, would steal rather than go home to be received with foul words and brutal blows.

This Avernus of the West is an area of vice. The most typical area of crime lies nearer to the City's heart. It has been said, "Wall off Hoxton, and nine-tenths of the criminals of London would be walled off." That is, perhaps, a too sweeping statement, but that there are whole areas in Hoxton inhabited entirely by criminals is a fact beyond dispute. Those criminals are principally thieves and burglars. The majority are of the lowest order, but there are among them several superior "artists"—men who plan and carry out big jobs. The "fences," or receivers of stolen goods, have made quite a little colony here, and the modern trainer of thieves, the Fagin of the twentieth century, has his daily and nightly classes in the neighbourhood.

Look at this row of neat-looking houses. There are blinds and well-arranged curtains at the windows, the handle of the bell is polished, the steps are clean. The signs without bespeak comfort within. These houses are largely occupied by the superior craftsmen in crime. One or two receivers also reside here, and the cleverest trainer of young thieves in London occupies the upper portion of the house that has the best show of flowers in the home-made window-boxes.

It has been my privilege to converse with some of these trainers and to get an insight into their methods. I am not betraying any confidence in publishing what I have learnt of their system, because it is perfectly well known to the police and to the Christian workers who labour among the pupils of the modern Fagin. The boy who is "trained" is, as a rule, taught one branch of the art of robbery only. For instance, a thief who wants to be an expert abstracter of ladies' watches never steals watches from men. If he "mixes his pockets" he loses his delicacy of touch. The fingers must be employed in one way in taking a watch from a man's pocket, and in quite another way in taking a watch from a lady. To steal from the person adroitly and with little fear of detection the fingers must be in constant practice in one particular way. Many a thief who has stolen from women for years with impunity has come to instant grief when, tempted by the apparent carelessness of the owner in a crowd, he has tried to take a watch from a man.

The most difficult branch of the "profession" for the young thief to learn is "counter creeping." To enter a shop on your hands and knees, crawl round behind the counter, and secure the till unnoticed by the shopkeeper requires the most skilful use, not only of the hands, but of the knees. The slightest sound as you crawl along the floor might attract attention. Yet, in spite of its difficulties, this branch of the business has many apprentices, who practise in a room in which an imitation counter is fitted up.

The "till sneak" occasionally acts with an accomplice, sometimes with two. When the favourable shop has been fixed upon, the habits of its owners studied, and the propitious moment chosen, one of the confederates enters as a pretended customer and engages the attention of the shopkeeper—frequently a woman. Another confederate keeps observation outside, and is ready to facilitate the exit of his "pals." The trained till thief creeps in and secures the haul noiselessly.

It often happens that the shopkeeper does not discover the loss until another customer has been served, and he or she goes to the till to put money in it and finds it empty.

But with all their cleverness, with all the risks they run in following their dishonest occupations, these professional thieves seem to make a very poor living.

If you would see how they live, let us go boldly into one of the criminal areas and enter the houses.

Here is the most notorious criminal street in London. The inhabitants are frankly thieves and of a very rough class. In the centre of the street is a lodging-house in which some two hundred thieves are accommodated nightly, and there is hardly a house from end to end in which the weekly rent is gained by honest industry.

Look at this "notice" chalked up in big letters on a wall: "Coppers wanted. Three killed last night."

That is a playful exaggeration. A policeman killed in this street a month or two ago, but only one. The whistle of a hooligan captain sounded, and scores of young roughs poured out of the houses to obey the summons. A "nark," or a lad who was suspected of "marking"—i.e. betraying a comrade by giving information to the police—had ventured into the neighbourhood, and the gang were called forth to administer lynch law. There was a big fight, for the suspected "nark" had pals too. In the course of the combat an unfortunate policeman so far forgot the first law of nature as to enter the street with a view of restoring order. He was so badly knocked about and injured that he died shortly afterwards.

If you enter the houses, which are mostly let at 12s. 6d. a week and taken by one person, who lets off the rooms and lives rent free in the process, you will find the most terrible squalor and apparent misery.

Most of the families live in one room. Occasionally, when one of the girls is old enough to do factory-work and bring home a regular wage, the luxury of two rooms is indulged in.

Here is a criminal family living in one room. There is a broken-down bedstead in the corner, and on it a dirty mattress and a patchwork quilt, originally of many colours, but now of one prevailing hue, that of greasy brown. There is not a chair or a table in the place. There are only a few broken and battered pails and tubs, which serve the purpose of chairs. In one of these tubs a baby is wedged in with rags, and in this position carried out and placed on the pavement. That is because the mother, who is alone, is going out, and there is a fire burning in the battered grate. The baby might play with the fire and burn the bed, and that would be a loss to the family. So the baby is deposited in the tub outside the front door, and left there for the hours that its mother has arranged to be absent.

If you were to enter this room in the small hours you would find it occupied by the grandmother, the mother and her husband, two young girls, and a lad of fifteen. There are two older lads in the family, but they are more comfortably lodged in one of His Majesty's prisons.

Here is the home of a professional burglar. He has only one room at present for himself, his wife, a lad of seventeen, two girls of fourteen and eight, and a baby. Presumably the burglary trade has shared in the general depression, for the family are at dinner when we enter, and it consists of nothing more appetizing than bread and cheese.

In one day I visited the homes of over fifty professional thieves in this district. This burglar was the only one who did not reciprocate my friendly advances. He was surly, and, but for the fact that circumstances compelled him to be civil to the friend who accompanied me, he would, I am sure, have given me a very unpleasant interview. In twenty of the houses I visited, a member was temporarily absent from the family circle. Some were away for six months, some for five years. There was no concealment as to their present address. "In prison," was the frank reply, sometimes made with a smile.

In only one instance was there any trepidation shown at the entry of unexpected visitors. That was when we went downstairs into a kitchen occupied by a middle-aged lady. Hearing strange footsteps, she had hastily attempted to conceal a bulky-looking sack under the bed. She explained her "palpitations" by assuring us that she suffered from heart disease.

As the lady was the wife of a gentleman who receives stolen goods, and has another kitchen at the back in which gold and silver articles are subjected to certain "transforming processes," we quite understood the nervousness which the lady betrayed, and her relief when we bade her good-bye and mounted the stairs again.

There are a dozen streets in this area, every one of them packed with criminals. But everywhere is the sign of squalor and penury. Walk through the streets, and you will see the children ragged, dirty, and barefooted. Nowhere in London is the note of misery so emphasized.

Crime, so far as these areas are concerned, must be a far less profitable occupation than the worst-paid class of honest labour.

And yet these people look solely to crime for their rent, their clothing, and their food, and wouldn't do an honest day's work if it were offered to them.

CHAPTER XVI
THE BLACK SHEEP

A sham funeral to hide shame—Moneylenders who discount forged bills —Was she responsible?—Haunted by a living spectre—At the mercy of a spendthrift—Where the father is the black sheep

NOT very long ago a high dignitary of the Church stood in the witness-box while his brother stood in the dock. Human endurance had come to an end, and the well-known divine had given his brother in charge to protect himself from violence and his family from insult.

This high dignitary of the Church was a man beloved and admired. No one who listened to his sermons, no one who saw him in his delightful home in the midst of his family, imagined that for years his life had been made miserable by the conduct of his own brother.

But at last the torture passed endurance, and the aid of the law was invoked. Then the skeleton in the family cupboard was dragged out into the light of day. But thousands of men and women in good positions set their teeth and bear the strain and the pain. They endure in silence and keep a smiling face before the world. The blacker the black sheep of the family is, the more earnestly they strive to avoid doing or saying anything which will draw public attention to the evil-doer.

It has happened in more than one case that the members of a noble family, stung to the quick by the infamy of one bearing their name, have connived at a false death and sham burial.

Such a case occurred some years ago, when, death being the only way to avoid a criminal trial, the relatives of the offender, who had fled to avoid arrest, gave out that he was dead, procured a body, and buried a stranger in the family vault.

With the supposed death of So-and-so the action which the outraged law had commenced against him ceased. The black sheep lay, so the world was informed, among his noble ancestors, beyond all human retribution. When the coffin that bore his name upon the plate was being lowered into the grave the black sheep was on his way to the East. There, under an assumed name, he lived for some years. It was not until his noble relatives received the news of his actual death through a faithful servant who had accompanied him into exile that they felt easy in their minds about him. They had always been haunted by the terror that in a fit of mad recklessness he would come back to England. He had threatened to do so more than once when the remittances were not as generous as he thought they should be.

There lay some little time back in the condemned cell of a London gaol a man who had committed a brutal murder for gain. The man was tried under a false name, and in that false name executed. For years he had been the black sheep of the family, sinking at last so low in his criminal career that his relatives refused to have anything more to do with him.

This man's real name was a well-known one in the world of philanthropy and the world of commerce. His friends, when they heard of his arrest for murder, were haunted by the fear that he might reveal his identity and put a public shame upon them.

But the murderer put their minds at ease in that regard. While awaiting trial he wrote to the head of the family informing him that he need be under no apprehension. Whatever the result of the trial might be, he, the prisoner, would retain the false name he had assumed when he first took to criminal courses. So perfectly was the secret of this murderer's identity kept that his mother, who died quite recently, never knew that her son had been tried for his life, found guilty, and executed.

But it is not often that the black sheep shows any consideration for the honour of his house. On the contrary, he trades upon the fear his kinsmen have of being injured by the exposure of his infamies. It is the knowledge of what the family will sacrifice to save the good name imperilled by one of its members that makes the money-lender discount without a word the acceptance that he knows to be a forgery.

A. Z. was the son of a retired colonel. He was a trouble to his people from his boyhood. Soon after he came of age a position was found for him in a City office. He led a fast life and gambled, got hold of his father's cheque-book, forged his father's signature, and obtained five hundred pounds. Then he confessed what he had done, and the father had to suffer the loss or allow his son to be criminally prosecuted by the bank.

He naturally made no communication to the bank, and the paid forged cheque was debited to his account.

Encouraged by his first success, A. Z., failing to get hold of his father's cheque-book again, forged the name of an acquaintance, a wealthy young man, to a bill and discounted it with a West End money-lender. The amount was a thousand pounds.

A week before the bill came due he left home and wrote his father a letter—apparently a broken-hearted, penitent letter—in which again he confessed his crime.

He entreated his father to see the young man whose signature had been forged and arrange the matter. The young man was the son of a brother officer of the old colonel's. He was horrified at the discovery of young Z.'s treachery, but he consented to receive the thousand pounds and take the bill up with it.

The colonel, in despair, told his daughters—he was a widower—what had happened. If their brother persisted in his evil courses there was nothing in front of the family but ruin and shame and humiliation. The little household was reduced to despair. Night and day they were haunted by the terror of what the black sheep would do next.

What he did, having squandered the whole of the money he had obtained by his last forgery, was to swindle tradespeople by giving worthless cheques.

In every instance he had stated who he was, and the colonel, being well known, was appealed to by the tradespeople, who did not want to prosecute if they could get their money.

Again the colonel paid, but his little capital had begun to be seriously diminished by these continued drains upon it.

"Father," said the eldest girl, as he described the terrible position in which her brother's conduct had placed them, "Arthur will ruin us. He will bring us to the gutter. So long as you have a farthing left in the world he will continue to rob you."

She brooded on it. She began to hate her brother, the cause of all their misery. She wished that he was dead.

A few months later the young man, as the result of the evil life he was living, was taken seriously ill. He was suffering from alcoholism, and a trained nurse was engaged, as it was not safe to leave him.

His sisters went to see him occasionally. One afternoon the elder sister called. The nurse wanted to go out for half an hour, and the sister offered to stay with the patient.

A quarter of an hour later the sister rushed suddenly downstairs calling for help. Her brother had suddenly jumped out of bed, rushed to the window, flung it open, and leapt out. The window was on the third floor. The young man was picked up dead.

At the inquest the nurse declared that such an accident ought not to have happened. Miss ——————— knew that her brother was likely to make for the window if not restrained—that was a common thing with cases of the kind. There was a bell in the room, and in the adjoining room was the sick man's male servant. There should not have been the slightest difficulty in restraining the would-be suicide, seeing that the window was fastened and assistance could have been secured in a moment.

The sister explained that she was so horrified when she saw her brother leap out of bed and make for the window she could do nothing. She nearly fainted. When she recovered herself her brother was through the window, and then she rushed out of the room calling for help.

But the fate of the black sheep saved the family. The relatives, who knew the story, have their own view of what happened. That which was a mystery to the hired nurse was no mystery to them. The sister deliberately let her brother go to his death.

It is not always the younger members of a family who are the black sheep. Sometimes it is the father—the mother—the husband—the wife.

In the days when a great music-hall star was at the height of his fame, and had fortune at his feet, I saw him in his charming home with his boy and his two little girls. The star had been an actor, and was a man of culture and education. He had been separated from his wife for some years. She had left him in circumstances which entirely released him from any moral responsibility with regard to her.

His early married life had been wrecked by this woman, who had become a dipsomaniac. After she left him he devoted himself to his three children. His delight was in them and in his home.

One night I was passing the music hall at which he was starring. His brougham was waiting for him at the stage door, and a little crowd had gathered to see him come out. He came, and there was a cheer, and at that moment a dissipated-looking woman, with a battered bonnet on her untidy hair, with torn dress and bedraggled skirts, reeled forward and caught him by the arm.

"Hulloa!" she shouted. "It's you, is it?"

The "star" went very white as he looked into the drunken woman's face. He shook himself free from her clutch and stepped hurriedly into the brougham.

The drunken woman yelled a volley of abuse after him as he drove away.

Then she turned to the crowd and exclaimed—

"I'm his wife—his lawful wife—curse him!—and that's how he treats me."

For ten years the terror of meeting this woman embittered the life of a great popular favourite. It was useless for him to give her money. It went in drink. He had once after she left him given her a home for herself. In six weeks she had sold every stick, and during that time she had twice been locked up and fined for being drank and creating a disturbance in the street.

She would meet him outside a hall, then disappear for months, to turn up again and publicly claim him as her husband before a crowd of people.

The woman died some years ago in a workhouse infirmary. In her last illness she said who she was, and the great music-hall star was communicated with. He bought a grave for her, and on the tombstone above it he had these words placed:

"Sacred to the memory of ———— —————, wife of ————— ————."

Dead, he could acknowledge her. Living, his haunting terror was that he might meet her, and she might call him husband.

In France, when the family fortune and the family honour are being imperilled by a member, a family council can be called, and can invoke the aid of the law to limit the powers of the offending individual. Here no such system exists. A man who has lost all moral control over himself may squander his substance and leave his children beggars. A young man succeeding to a considerable estate may get rid of it in insane extravagance in a year or two. A widow left with the control of her dead husband's fortune may embark on foolish speculations or become the dupe of swindlers and leave the sons and daughters of her dead husband without a farthing in the world.

Mr. B————, who had a high financial position in the City, died and left a widow and four children, all girls. Fortunately, he settled a small sum on each of the girls, but the bulk of his fortune went to the widow.

She was forty-two when her husband died; the eldest girl was nineteen and the youngest fourteen.

Soon after her widowhood Mrs. B———— took to drink. Now began a purgatory for the daughters. The mother would go out every morning and be absent all day. At night she would return staggering, helpless, hopelessly intoxicated.

Sometimes she would be brought home by a policeman. One night a constable found her just before midnight lying on her own doorstep with a black bag in her hand. The black bag, which was half open, contained £700 in notes and gold. The unhappy woman had been to the bank in the afternoon and cashed a cheque for £800. A hundred pounds was missing. What had become of it she herself when she became sober was unable to say. She couldn't remember.

So things went on for two years. Night after night these young girls sat in their home listening to every footstep, waiting for their mother to return.

One night she did not come home at all. The next morning they heard she had been locked up. The police had found her lying in the street with a large sum of money on her, and had locked her up for her own safety.

In her home her presence was often more terrible than her absence. In her delirium she would threaten to kill her daughters. The terrified girls would lock themselves in a bedroom and remain there sometimes for days together, fearing their mother's violence.

In her right senses she loved her children tenderly, and then she was the best of mothers. But as time went on her intervals of sanity became rarer and rarer.

The first day of peace these poor young ladies knew was that on which they followed their mother to her grave.

Mr. H——— has two sons, one a well-known barrister, the other a physician. Both have won for themselves a position in the world. But both have one great and constant terror. Their father is the black sheep of the family.

Up to the age of fifty Mr. H——— was a merchant of repute in the City. He had apparently an ample fortune, and he brought his children up in luxury. His wife died when he was fifty-one, and a year after he became involved in a long and expensive lawsuit.

Soon afterwards a remarkable change came over him. He neglected his business, made questionable acquaintances, and began to drink heavily. Then his affairs became involved. The business was given up. He sold his house and went to live in chambers. All his children had previously left him; the girls had married, the sons were established—one, as I have said, being a barrister, the other a doctor.

One day, calling at his father's chambers, the barrister was astonished to learn that he had given them up and gone away.

The family were alarmed, knowing something of their

The missing merchant was discovered living in a low-class foreign hotel in Soho.

He gave no explanation of his conduct, but allowed himself to be taken to his son's house—the doctor's.

Some time afterwards the doctor was astonished on returning home to find a man in possession of his home. The man had been put in for a debt of £600 which the merchant had contracted, stating that the house—the doctor's—was his residence.

The doctor, with the aid of a solicitor, got rid of the bailiff, and eventually to avoid a scandal he and the barrister paid the £600 between them.

A month later the doctor found another man in possession, this time for £100. His father had borrowed a hundred of a money-lender, giving his son's address as his own.

An investigation made showed that the once prosperous merchant had so hopelessly involved his affairs that he was practically without resources, and it was impossible to ascertain what liabilities he was incurring.

In five years the sons between them paid over £10,000 to avoid the scandal which would have arisen had their father's peculiar business transactions come into court.

For both of them life had become a constant harass and strain. They could not prevent their father getting credit by publicly advertising that he had no resources. Such a course would have brought about the very publicity they were anxious to avoid.

And the father, finding that the sons eventually paid on every occasion, however much they protested at first, continued to incur liabilities. Many of his transactions were morally insane if not legally so.

One of his last feats was to sign an acceptance for £500 and give it to a man he met in the smoking-room of an hotel to get discounted for him. He and this man divided the proceeds between them. He was introduced to his new financial agent one Monday afternoon by somebody whose name he forgot, and on Tuesday he handed him the bill.

This time, when proceedings were taken on the bill, the sons father's newly-developed habits, and inquiries were made.

But certain allegations were made, and, to avoid "unpleasantness," they compounded and paid £300 to get the bill back.

When I last heard of the black sheep father he had been "converted," and was thinking of joining the Salvation Army.

The sons are nervous. They have an idea that they will one day meet their father in a scarlet uniform beating a big drum.

But even that would be a relief, if he devotes himself to music and abandons finance.

In the lives of the people lie the Mysteries of modern London, and the Black Sheep go to the making of many of them.

CHAPTER XVII
CHILDREN AND CRIME

The hereditary taint—Cain, as a child of fifteen—Because he wouldn't give her a toy—Playing with fire—A heartless lie for a threepenny-bit—Suicide among children

THERE is one phase in the mystery of life in the great City which I would gladly pass. But it is one of the strangest, one of the least known, and it is impossible to ignore it.

Only those whose duties or whose studies bring them into contact with the saddest phase of child-life in London know how terrible is the picture that could be painted by an artist who, in his desire for realism, did not shrink from the most painful details.

It is not my desire, nor is it the purpose of these chapters, to take the darkest view of the sins and sorrows of the City.

The truth—the appalling truth—concerning the phase to which I am now referring is written in the records of the schools in which the feeble-minded children of London are specially cared for and dealt with. In these volumes the family history of the parents of every child is written, the doctor's view of the child's mental and physical condition is given, and nothing that can be ascertained for the guidance of the teachers is left unrecorded.

The authorities have decided—and very wisely decided—that these volumes shall be bound with metal clasps and locked from the eyes of all save those who have by their official position the right of access to them.

There are some terrible family histories in those guarded volumes. The sins of the parents are there, and the children on whom the sins have been visited are in the schools for the mentally and physically unfit.

Not always is it sin that has set its mark upon the offspring. Drink has much to answer for in the deterioration of a race; but here there is affliction as well—degenerate parents have married and given the world degenerate children.

Insanity, epilepsy, all the forms of mental instability contribute to the legion of the lost little ones.

If you could see the record of the parents you would find again and again that suicide and insanity had occurred in the family. You would find weak-minded parents with six and seven children—sometimes with ten. Out of one family of ten that I know only two of the children are normal. Through the generations the taint has been handed down, and that is the reason that lunacy is advancing by leaps and bounds, and the number of the insane is now so great that even the unthinking are beginning to be alarmed.

I am not going to point a moral here or to urge a reform. This is not the place. But I have been compelled to state the truth that the reason for the existence in our midst of a class of children who are dangerous to the community may be understood.

Here is a lad of fifteen. A few months ago the law decided that the time had come when the freedom of the home and the streets shall be denied him, and that he shall be kept where the commission of further crimes by him will be guarded against.

This lad of fifteen attempted to murder a little boy of six. He met the boy in the streets, took him to a lonely place, and there savagely attacked him. The child succeeded in escaping from the homicidal maniac of fifteen, who later on was arrested and charged at the police-court.

There, when it became a question of the boy's sanity, a circumstance was narrated to the magistrate which threw a lurid light on the case.

A year previously the boy had taken his little sister of four for a walk. Two hours later he returned to his home saying that the child had fallen into the canal and was drowned.

Search was made, and the body of the child was found in the water. But to get there she had had to force her body through some broken palings, and portions of her clothing were found on this side of them.

The tragedy passed at the time as an accident. It was supposed the child in childish heedlessness had got through the palings and fallen in.

There is no doubt in the minds of those who knew the children that the little girl was deliberately thrust into the canal by her then fourteen-year-old brother. The boy was a homicidal maniac. His one idea was to take life. After he had been taken to an asylum many things came to light. Other children came forward and told how he had suddenly seized them in quiet places, and how, terrified by his strange look and his violent actions, they had struggled and escaped, and fled from him in terror.

The piano is being played in this big schoolroom, and some fifty little girls are taking part in the musical drill, which is part of their course of instruction. Many of them are pretty and neatly dressed, but there is a strange, uncanny look in some of the faces. Yet they are dangerous, requiring on the part of their teachers the utmost vigilance. Some of them become furiously angry in a moment, and if a schoolfellow is the cause of their anger will burst into fits of uncontrollable rage and threaten vengeance. Others are cunning and wait for their opportunity.

One of these girls, annoyed at having to mind a baby sister in what she considered her playtime, took it out with her, went some distance from home, and left the mite under a dark railway arch near a piece of waste ground. Then she came back and said that while she was out walking a big woman had snatched the baby and run away with it.

Fortunately, some one passing the arch soon afterwards heard a child cry, went in and found the baby, and was taking it to the police-station when she met the mother, who had gone in search of it.

The girl had stated that it was on the waste ground that the woman had attacked her, and this led the mother to search in that direction.

Another of these girls—a pretty little maid of twelve—invented a blood-curdling story which caused the utmost consternation in the neighbourhood. She declared that she had seen a man kill two children and throw them into the canal. She described the man, and declared that it was a half-witted, inoffensive hawker known as "Jim," who sometimes came about the neighbourhood selling little halfpenney home-made toys to the children.

The next time "Jim" was seen he had a very bad quarter of an hour, and might have been lynched if a policeman passing by had not come to the rescue and heard the story. The child was then cross-examined, and, apparently frightened by the policeman, said it wasn't "Jim," but somebody very like him.

Some time afterwards it was ascertained that the girl had invented the story for the deliberate purpose of getting "Jim" set upon and "hurt." He had refused to let her have a toy that she fancied for nothing.

Here in a mean street in the neighbourhood of the old "Nichol," immortalized by Mr. Arthur Morrison, is a small four-roomed house. It is occupied by one family who, in this neighbourhood, would be considered well off.

The head of the family is a man of forty-five. He is of weak intellect and has epileptic fits. He has an income of a week, derived from property left him by a relative. The sum is paid to him weekly by a solicitor. His wife is older. She married him "for his money," and spends as much as she can get in drink. There are five children at home. There were seven. The two absent are little boys—one of four and one of six. The little boy of four is dead. He went out for a walk with the boy of six one morning and never came back. The elder boy said that his little brother had run away. The next day a woman, going to her dustbin, which stood in her little bit of front garden, was horrified, on lifting the lid, to find the dead body of a little boy. The elder boy had throttled the younger and put the body in the dustbin. When the tragedy was inquired into the child said that "something told him to do it."

This Cain of six is now in an asylum for idiots. When he gets his liberty he will, if he refrains from further criminal violence, grow up and marry and have a family.

There is no sadder sight than—with a knowledge of this terrible phase of child-life—to watch these poor little degenerates come trooping out of the schools where a brave endeavour is being made to save them from the consequences of their own mental and moral deficiency.

Yes, there is one thing more painful still—that is, to listen to the prayers of their unhappy parents that the children of whom they are afraid—yes, literally afraid—may be taken from them and "put away."

"I never know a moment's peace," wailed one unhappy mother. "That boy has threatened to kill his little sister—and I'm sure that sooner or later he will do it."

Among these unfortunate children arson is a favourite amusement. Most children have a desire to play with fire, but here the object is distinctly mischievous. There is an intention to destroy property heedless of consequences, heedless even of the risk to human life.

"We shall be burned in our beds by him," said a poor woman one day to the schoolmistress. "He's set the place afire times when my back was turned, and the other day he got a lot of paper and shavings together and lighted 'em *under the cradle.*"

The hatred or jealousy of the baby is a painful feature in many of these cases. It is the jealousy of a mind that is feeble. This jealousy led a young girl of gentle birth to commit a murder which attained world-wide notoriety.

Constance Kent killed her baby brother because she was jealous of him. There are several Constance Kents among these mentally deficient children, and many a baby meets with a fate which is supposed to be accidental, but the accident was materially contributed to by a brother or a sister.

For some of these children certain objects have an irresistible fascination.

There is no story more remarkable than that of the boy of fourteen in Paris who had murdered first an old woman and then an old man, solely in older to get possession of the cheap watches they wore.

After the boy's arrest several watches were found concealed in his home. They had no money value to him. He was simply collecting watches, and did not hesitate to kill in order to add to the number.

To get possession of some trifling and valueless ornament, a string of beads, a penny brooch, a toy, a few marbles, young children of the unfortunate class I am dealing with have laid the most elaborate plans. One youthful desperado noticed that a little girl on Sundays wore a string of beads to which was attached a lucky threepenny-bit—a threepenny-bit with a hole in it.

The child was always with an elder sister on Sundays, and there was no chance of a highway robbery. Moreover, the children knew the boy, and if he snatched the necklace they would tell their parents who did it.

He wormed himself into the confidence of the children, and ascertained that on week-days the necklace was kept put away in a drawer in the bedroom with the Sunday clothes.

On that information he acted. One day, when only the mother was at home, the sisters being out playing in another street near the school, the young hopeful suddenly rushed into her room. "Oh, Mrs. Jones," he exclaimed, "there's a little girl been run over in the next street, and I think it's your Annie!"

Off went Mrs. Jones, and the boy instantly made his way into the bedroom, found the drawer, opened it, and abstracted the necklace with the lucky threepenny-bit on it.

In all the cases that I know of childish criminality of the insane type—none of these children are of normal intellect—there is a family history which accounts for everything.

In the case of a little lad who broke into a house for the sole purpose of killing a canary—and he killed it cruelly—the mother and father were "afflicted," and the eight children of the family were all of violent temper and a source of constant annoyance to the neighbours. Six of them had been certified for "special instruction"—i.e., to be sent to the schools specially arranged for the feeble-minded.

It was for a long time a widely entertained idea that for a great deal of juvenile crime the sensational stories called "Penny Dreadfuls" were largely responsible.

In the worst cases of juvenile crime—or, it would be fairer to say, of juvenile insanity with a criminal tendency—of which I have had personal knowledge, there has been no fiction reading at all. The appeal to the imagination has been wholly lacking. The children have acted on their own initiative or the suggestion of a companion suffering from a similar lack of moral sense.

Here are two boys who broke into a church—one is fourteen, the other fifteen. Their object was to get at the offertory box in which they had seen money placed. On the younger boy when he was caught was found a common table-knife which he had taken from his home.

Asked what he had taken the knife with him for, he said without the slightest hesitation, "To stick into anybody that tried to nab me."

It was fortunate for the policeman who caught the lad as he came out of the church that he seized his quarry by both arms; otherwise he might have had practical proof of what the knife was carried for.

Suicide among children is officially announced to be on the increase. Suicide among children—the idea is terrible! One can hardly connect childhood with deliberate self-destruction. How, one asks oneself, can a child have become so melancholy, so depressed, so weary of life as to seek that which for all normal children has an element of terror in it—death?

The answer is that a large number of attempts at suicide by children are not caused by melancholia, but by insane malice or ungovernable temper. The dominant idea is the idea of causing trouble and pain to others. A little girl who attempted to commit suicide by throwing herself into a canal explained after she had been rescued that she did it to *upset her mother*.

I have dwelt reluctantly on this feature of our modern life—this outcome of the stress of civilization. I have made no mention of one phase of it with which the police-courts are, unfortunately, only too familiar. For its details you must turn to the records of rescue homes in which the cases are set out of girls of tender years who have been "rescued." But it is impossible to ignore the feature itself in dealing with the mysteries, or little-known phases, of London life.

The extent of the evil is not appreciated by the great public, for they see little of it. Even if they were to see a hundred of these children learning in the schools or romping in the playground, ordinary observers would not suspect the tragedy that lies below the surface.

For each of these children is a human document—a document which the genius of a Zola could extend into a world-shocking realistic romance like "L'Assommoir," or "Nana."

In the locked and guarded volumes where the family histories of these children are recorded lie more horrors than ever the great French novelist dared to blacken his pages with. There are the first and the second chapters of life-stories that ere they are closed will add many a strange romance of passion and crime, of madness and murder, to the mysteries of the town.

CHAPTER XVIII
BEHIND BRICK WALLS

Some who have tried and failed—A disgrace to the family—A tragedy of mirth—Living and dead as room-mates—A strange kind of kleptomania—A pathetic story of fidelity

WHEN the interior of a house is set upon the stage, the offers harbourage to the fair frail craft that almost at the outset show signs of the storm through which they have passed before they made the harbour. About a third of them are London born, the others came from the quiet country to the city paved with gold, and in its glitter and glamour were lost.

The fourth wall is always down in order that the audience may see what is going on. In real life the dramas within the domestic interior are played with the fourth wall up. Sometimes through the windows we may catch a passing glance of domestic comedy, but when it comes to drama, care is taken that no passer-by shall have a free entertainment.

I am going to take the fourth wall down to-day, not only of a private house here and there, but of certain public and philanthropic institutions. The Londoner out and about passes scores of such buildings in an ordinary day's walk and hardly notices them. He has no thought of the strange romances, of the dramatic mysteries, which lie behind the dull brick walls.

Here in a busy thoroughfare is an excellent institution which of life's voyage have been driven on the rocks of sin and shame, or have drifted perilously near to them.

Though it is known by another name, I will call it a Rescue Home, for its work is the rescue of young women in peril of evil, and the sheltering of those who, having fallen, need a friendly and protecting hand to save them from being engulfed in the depths.

It is an ordinary-looking house. There is nothing about it to attract attention; nothing to suggest the mighty war between the evil and the good that is being waged behind its dull brick walls.

If we enter we shall find young girls and young women going about the work and occupation of the day silently and soberly. All are young, some are pretty, some are haggard and wan.

A large number are of the servant class. Of 106 who were inmates of this home during one year, 74 had been in domestic service, and of these 65 had been "generals." The predominance of this class is accounted for by the fact that 99 of the 106 had "wandered and lost their way" between the ages of fourteen and twenty-one. Of the remainder, 5 were factory hands, 8 laundry workers, 2 sempstresses, and 2 girls still at school.

Many of the girls had tried to regain the right path, and failed because of their friendlessness. Some of them had homes, but the doors were closed against them.

Look at this frail, pale girl of eighteen. There is a look in the sad brown eyes raised to yours as you pass her at her work which goes straight to your heart. She is a girl who, penitent and broken-hearted, wrote to her father, imploring him to let her return to her home. Here is the letter she received in reply to her despairing appeal:—

"Bessie,—We are surprised to think that you should ever have the cheek to write to us again and to think we should give you another chance. I think you have had a good chance, and we do not intend to give you any more—in fact, if you dare to come and see us we will shut the door in your face, for you are a disgrace to the family..., You said that you wanted to go your own way; now you can go your own way.... You need not take the trouble ever to write to us again, for if you do it will be sent back unopened; at the same time you know if ever I should meet you it won't be good for you."

But all the inmates are not of the ordinary class. With regard to some of them there is a mystery that is never penetrated. That they are of superior birth and education they cannot conceal, but for the rest they are silent.

Not long since in this Home, at the hour when the Ladies' Committee was sitting, a visitor came who particularly wished to see them.

Shown in, she handed to the Committee a bank-note for £20, and to the surprise of every one explained that it was a thank-offering. A few years previously this charming and beautifully dressed lady had been herself an inmate of the Institution. She told her story frankly.

In a moment of temptation she had quitted her home, leaving no word behind which would enable her parents to trace her.

Her wilful course led her down step by step until she found herself an outcast from decent society, and she was then ashamed to let her friends know of her whereabouts.

One night she came to the Refuge and applied for admission. She was taken in, and after eighteen months' training she was placed in domestic service. Shortly afterwards, in quite a remarkable way, her father discovered her and took her home. Her father was a man of wealth, holding a high position in Society.

When the "rescued" woman left the institution she was seen to enter a carriage, which had been waiting a few doors lower down. The coachman and footman were in aristocratic liveries, and had powdered hair.

What writer of fiction would have placed in a refuge for fallen women a girl who, while she was training there for domestic service, had a father whose men-servants wore powdered hair?

But behind the brick walls that strange romance was being worked out, and the mystery of the girl's identity remains unsolved to this day.

Here is a house that looks like a private residence, standing in its own grounds. There is a wall in front of it, and the door in this wall is solid and shuts out a view of the garden.

It stands in a broad, busy thoroughfare, and thousands of people pass it daily on foot or by 'bus and tram. They glance at the house carelessly, perhaps, but very few of them know what lies behind the hiding walls.

Here not long ago, in the shady garden, sat a monarch of merriment, a lord of laughterland, a bright comedian who had won world-wide fame, and whose quips and cranks had made the nation gay. He was beloved by all who love honest mirth. He was the idol of the people. And behind the high wall he sat day after day, haunted by morbid fancies, a prey to strange delusions, now singing a snatch of some old song of his that had echoed round the world, now imagining that once again he was travelling with a little show, and had to wheel his "props" and his baggage on a truck from the station to the little hall in which the evening show was to take place. Sometimes he would be patronizing, and generously bestow a knighthood or a baronetcy on an attendant. One day he would raise the kindly doctor who had charge of him to the peerage, and the next, forgetting that he had thousands at the bank, he would worry about some imaginary financial difficulty involving a few pounds.

He left this retreat after a time, cured, it was supposed, and once more the public thronged to see him, and to laugh at his jokes and antics, and to cheer him frantically. Alas! it was but a temporary lifting of the cloud. There was a relapse, and then the end came swiftly and mercifully.

I never see the pleasant retreat and look at the sheltering wall but I think of the delightful droll whom I knew and loved, and who passed the months of his madness here, his presence unsuspected by the thousands who passed by. They little thought what a train of mirth lay hidden away behind the few yards of brick.

Here, in a mean street in a poor district, is a house let out in rooms. In the lower front room the ragged dirty blind is down. From this house you will see in a couple of hours, if you wait and watch, a grand funeral procession start. There will be an open car drawn by a pair of horses, and on it will be a wreath-laden coffin. Funeral coaches and four-wheel cabs will follow with many mourners, and the street will be filled with a crowd of women and children assembled to see the grand funeral of Widow Wilson's eldest son.

While you are waiting for the funeral car and carriages to arrive, I will take down the fourth wall. Now you can see inside the room with the drawn blind.

It is a poverty-stricken, squalid room. In the centre is a rickety table, round which the widow and her three remaining children are gathered, making a scanty meal before they put on their black to follow the dead lad to the cemetery. The thin stew has been taken from the fire, and is being served out on chipped and cracked plates to the children, and in the centre of the table at which the family are dining lies the corpse.

I am not inventing the details to paint a picture of life among the poor—I am giving the actual facts as discovered by the School Board officer of the district, who called to inquire why one of the children had not attended school the previous day.

No one seeing the elaborate and expensive funeral that started a couple of hours later from the house could have imagined the scene there was to be witnessed behind the brick wall. The living and the dead had been together in that one room for over a week.

There are many reasons why funerals are not hurried in the poorer districts. Here is a case in which one was delayed for three weeks.

Mrs. Jones's baby died just as it was completing its first year's experience of life. Mr. Jones drew the money from the burial club and gave an order to the undertaker. But before the day fixed for the funeral arrived Mr. Jones had lost half the money by backing horses that didn't win. In his distress he spent the balance at the public-house. "No money, no funeral," was the undertaker's motto, so the baby uncoffined, but shrouded in a sheet, was left in the cupboard.

Mrs. Jones, when the disaster was made known to her, told her story to her poor neighbours. They generously clubbed together, and in a few days they handed her the needed amount.

In her gratitude Mrs. Jones invited a few of her neighbours, who had not subscribed, to drink the health of those who had.

The health-drinking affected Mrs. Jones so much that returning home she was absent-minded, and the balance of the funeral money was stolen from her by a thief who had followed her out of the public-house.

The body lay in the cupboard for another week, and the news of the delayed funeral reaching the authorities, an official called, and baby was at last taken away and buried by the parish.

That was the greatest punishment that could have been inflicted on the parents.

If a modern Asmodeus, instead of lifting the roof, would take us around London and remove the fourth walls, we should be astonished at the tragedy, or moved to laughter by the farcical comedy, that would be suddenly revealed.

If, for instance, the wall were down to-night in front of this "desirable residence" in a West End square, we should see into the bedroom of the son of the house.

The family have retired for the night. Up in his own room the son, a good-looking, elegant, and cultured young man of five-and-twenty, is gloating over his treasures.

He has locked his door, and now he is contemplating with the most intense satisfaction several sets of false teeth which he has arranged on a little table in front of him.

His own teeth are sound and white. He has no need for false ones. Why, then, has he bought twenty sets?

He has not purchased them. He has stolen them.

His peculiar form of kleptomania is appropriating false teeth. He steals them whenever he has a chance. He abstracts them from the door-cases of dentists, from the shops in which they are displayed. He would not dream of being dishonest in any other way, but false teeth have an irresistible fascination for him.

If we were to take down the wall of a still more aristocratic residence we might see a lady of title opening a drawer and carefully counting her large store of serviettes. The astonishing thing about her collection is that the monograms are all different.

Wherever this lady lunches or dines she secures a serviette, puts it in her pocket, and takes it home to add to her vast assortment.

The young man could afford to buy the false teeth he fancies so much; the titled lady could buy serviettes all day long without feeling the outlay. But both prefer to *steal* the article that they have a strange desire to possess.

We will look through one more brick wall before we finish our present trip.

Once more it is a "Rescue Home" in front of which we pause. The wall is down, and we see into a well-ordered house, in which a number of young women are engaged in various occupations.

Look well at that short, pale-faced girl, whose features bear traces of the life she has lived, the sorrow she has known.

She is going about her work quietly, silently, mechanically. You would think to look at her that she had been a general servant of the "slavey" type in some poor household. As a matter of fact she described herself, when the police demanded her occupation, as a "charwoman."

But the girl is only twenty-one now, and probably never did a day's "charring" in her life, unless she would so describe the occasional tidying up of the room in which she once lived as the companion of a young professional burglar.

A short time ago I saw this girl at the Old Bailey trying to save the life of her lover by committing perjury. I have never witnessed a more pathetic scene.

The great beads of agony stood on the girl's brow as she looked at the youth on his trial for murder, and endeavoured to retract the damning admissions she had previously made to the police—admissions which led to her lover's arrest, and practically put the rope round his neck.

The law has laid the man in a murderer's grave within the prison walls. The girl a few days before his execution bore a dead child.

In two months of her young life she sounded the deepest depths of human tragedy. She has known a torture and a despair which few women of her age have been fated to endure.

But in this quiet home she is being cared for and tended, and noble-hearted women are waiting and hoping for the moment when she can be given the chance of a better life.

In the pocket of the dress she wears there are two letters carefully wrapped up in thick paper to preserve them. They are the last letters her murderer lover wrote her. She will treasure them all her life.

If in the early days of the trial we could have removed the wall of the prison in which the man was confined we should have seen him scratching the girl's portrait on the door of his cell with the point of a common pin, and labelling her with a word that expressed his anger against her for telling the truth about him when she fell into the hands of the police.

He is dead, but behind the grey walls upon which we are gazing to-day is the life tragedy of the girl he left behind him.

CHAPTER XIX
THE SOCIAL MASK

Masks with a purpose—For the sake of their daughter—A murderer's smiling mask—Waiting for the convict son—A secret from his wife—Beaten in a fight with fate

THERE is a mask that most of us wear occasionally. It is not always politic to show ourselves to the world exactly as we are. People of the highest respectability, of the most irreproachable honour, find the same difficulty in avoiding the occasional use of the social mask that the good bishop found in systematically avoiding the evasive answer.

The smile with which you greet an acquaintance who calls upon you when his visit is most inconvenient is a social mask; so is the admiration you express for the "dear little children" of your hostess when they are worrying you to death.

But that is not quite the social mask that I have in mind at the present time. I propose to deal rather with the men and women who wear the social mask to conceal from the world something of far greater importance than dislike, contempt, or weariness.

The social mask of wealth is often worn to conceal poverty; of extravagance to conceal bankruptcy; of love to conceal hatred; of gaiety to conceal grief; of innocence to conceal guilt.

If something happened which compelled the social mask to be laid aside by all our acquaintances, the revelation would astonish us; for it is worn in every rank of life and by all sorts and conditions of men and women.

Only in the home—sometimes only when the door of the room in which the wearer can be alone is locked—is the mask laid aside.

The husband may wear it for years in the presence of his wife; the wife may wear it in the presence of the husband.

Both wear a mask unsuspected by the other until the day that death dissolves their union.

There died not long ago a man who was universally esteemed and respected. He was looked upon as a model husband and father. His married life had been unclouded by a domestic care. His widow in her time of grief spoke of him as the truest, kindest husband that ever a woman had.

But for years he had worn a mask. He had not been in his grave a fortnight before the startling discovery was made that the man without reproach had another wife and another family and another home, and the two homes were not half a mile apart.

This man had worn the mask with both wives and both families. He had appeared to both to be all that was noble and good and constant in his affection. His profession being one that must necessarily take him from home pretty frequently to various parts of the country, he had been able to carry on the deception without arousing suspicion on either side. A clever arrangement of sending letters into the country to be posted back to his wives had got over the difficulties of correspondence during the intervals.

Husbands and wives who have long ceased to find pleasure in each other's society often wear the mask for the children's sake. Before the world and before their guests they are still a happy, united couple, but the marriage tie is a prison fetter to them both.

In a fashionable church the other day an aristocratic crowd assembled to witness the marriage of a beautiful girl, the only daughter of a couple well known in Society. No word of scandal had ever been whispered against husband or wife. At the wedding reception hopes were fervently expressed by old friends of the family that the married life of the fair young bride might be as happy as that of her parents. The young husband and wife drove away, and then one by one the guests bade the smiling father and mother good-bye.

The next day the smiling parents separated, each to make a separate home. The tragedy of their lives was over—or, if you will, the farce was finished. For ten years they had not spoken a kindly word to each other except in public. But that nothing might spoil or interfere with the matrimonial chances of their daughter they had worn the mask of a loyal and loving union.

A young man of fashion, elegant, good-looking, admired, and credited with the enjoyment of everything that goes to make life worth living! It was my privilege to know him, and I never saw him without a smile. One afternoon he came into the club, looked round the room, saw a friend, and invited him to play billiards.

The friend was not that way inclined, so the young man of fashion joined a little group and presently he was making us all merry. He was the embodiment of the joy of life, and more than one of us envied him his perennial flow of animal spirits.

He left the club and went home to his chambers, put a pistol to his head and blew his brains out, leaving behind him a note to say that he was unable any longer to endure the torture his life had become to him.

It was not until some months afterwards that we knew what had induced him to commit suicide. The woman he loved had married another man. The marriage took place in June, the suicide in September, so that for three months this young man had worn the mask of gaiety while his heart was slowly breaking.

The murderer and the murderess do not as a rule go about allowing their features to express their guilt. There are many crimes yet to be discovered; many which never, perhaps, will be discovered, the authors of which are going about among their fellow-citizens, keeping up appearances, and passing for very amiable and worthy people.

Wainwright, who murdered Harriett Lane, had the reputation of being "a good fellow." He had excellent social qualities, and was always welcomed by his acquaintances because of his good spirits and cheery views of life.

All the time that the body of the woman he had murdered was lying under the floor of his warehouse in Whitechapel, Henry Wainwright was earning golden opinions of all sorts of people. He was highly appreciated as a temperance lecturer, and of many a family gathering or festival he was the life and soul. And all the time the terror of discovery was gnawing at his heart. Shortly after his arrest I met a man who had been his intimate friend for years. He told me that on the last occasion they spent an evening together he had asked Wainwright how he managed always to look so supremely happy. Wainwright did not tell him that the smile was a mask he wore to impose on society. He said instead that he was happy because he had a good digestion and a clear conscience.

A friend and *confrère* of mine had a cook-housekeeper—a middle-aged woman whose smiling good humour made her a general favourite.

One day a man of fifty-five was arrested for the murder of the woman with whom he lived, and who was supposed to be his wife.

This man was tried, convicted, and executed.

On the morning of the execution the housemaid came to my *confrère's* room in a state of great excitement and told him that the housekeeper had fallen down "suddenly all of a heap," and was in a dead faint.

When the master went downstairs he found the poor woman had recovered and was sitting in a chair. She was very white and ill, and when he spoke kindly to her she began to cry.

He sent the other servants out of the room and asked her what was the matter.

Then, feeling probably that she *must* confide in some one, she told him the truth. The man who had that morning been hanged was her husband. He had deserted her for the other woman six years previously, and she had not seen him since.

She had read of the murder, the arrest, and the conviction, and with a great effort had concealed the agony the tragedy had caused her.

She had gone about her work smiling and amiable as ever, and it was only on the day that she knew her husband was dying on the gallows that the tension proved too much for her heart-strings and she broke down and let the mask fall.

A sweet-faced, white-haired old lady came to me a few weeks ago and asked me to sign a petition to the Home Secretary for the release of her son, who, many years ago, murdered a woman who had driven him to desperation. The young man was condemned to death, but the capital sentence was commuted to penal servitude for life.

I knew the young man, I knew his father and mother.

The father died. The old lady took her son's children, moved into a new neighbourhood, and brought them up in ignorance of the tragedy that had shadowed their lives.

I have seen the children, now grown up, happy in the home that granny has made for them. They have never read in that gentle, loving face the story of the sorrow that shattered her happiness for ever. To them granny is the embodiment of great happiness. She has set herself the task of brightening their lives and keeping the shadows away.

I hope and believe that the petition for her son's release will presently be granted. Then the father, whom the children believe to be far away engaged in business on the other side of the world and unable to leave it, will suddenly appear among them. He will have come home at last. But the secret so carefully guarded will be kept to the end. The children will never know that all these years their gentle, smiling, loving granny has worn a mask before them and before the world, and that night after night, when they could not see her, she has wept bitter tears for the son who was sentenced to death, and spared to work out a life sentence within the walls of a convict gaol.

The Humbert case startled the world. A family on the brink of a volcano of shame and humiliation lived gaily and grandly, imposing upon the cleverest and shrewdest men in Europe. In their case suspicion was aroused before the final crash came, and the famous safe was found to be empty.

But we have our Humberts here in London, concerning whom not the slightest suspicion exists. We see them living in luxury, indulging in the most lavish hospitality, and fêted everywhere in return.

Less fortunate people envy them, perhaps, for their wealth. No one guesses that they are hopelessly involved, and that their life is a perpetual stress and harass because they are compelled to scheme from morning to night in order to continue the imposture and postpone the fatal day of discovery, which is rapidly approaching.

When that day comes the head of the family will have his choice between the pistol or poison of the suicide and the dock of the Old Bailey.

The hero, or, rather, I should say the villain, of one of the most sensational frauds of modern times was princely in his hospitality. His wife, to celebrate their little boy's birthday, which was at Christmas time, gave a children's party, and there was a Christmas tree. I was a child at the time, and one of my playmates, a little boy who lived a few doors from me, was invited. He brought home a beautiful little gold watch, which he said had been given him from the Christmas tree. His mother, concluding that some mistake must have been made, took the watch back. With considerable haughtiness the hostess explained that no mistake had been made. "There was nothing on our Christmas tree worth less than five pounds," she said; "that was the lowest." Three months afterwards the haughty lady's husband was sentenced to fifteen years' penal servitude for a series of frauds in which nearly half a million of money was involved. For years he had worn the mask of generosity over the face of a rascal.

He confessed after his conviction that for months before his arrest he had been in hourly dread of discovery, and there were times when he contemplated suicide. Yet not even his wife had the shadow of a suspicion that he had not legitimately acquired the wealth he spent so ostentatiously.

A genial and widely respected solicitor has just retired into convict life for a period of years. Up to the day of his arrest he was looked upon as the most charming of men, and was a welcome guest at some of the best country houses. His manners were delightful and his light-hearted gaiety infectious. It was known that he was backing an enterprise that had failed, and lost large sums of money in it. But everybody said, "What does it matter to him? He is so rich. It evidently hasn't upset him—he's as jolly as ever."

But the genial and gentlemanly solicitor had been using trust money. He wore the mask until sentence was pronounced. It was much more severe than he anticipated. When he heard it he buried his face in his hands and wept in the dock.

It is a May meeting at Exeter Hall. All the people crowded together to listen to the speeches from the platform love their fellow-men. There are clergymen and philanthropists, bright old ladies and serious young ones all listening with rapt attention to the genial eloquence of a gentleman honoured for his good works and his philanthropy.

It is a beautiful speech, and the face of the speaker beams with benevolence.

You would not think to look at that kindly, smiling face, that the speaker had a care in the world. But follow him home. See him when, his doors closed against the outside world, he drops the mask.

He could smile at others. He cannot smile to himself. The terror of the future is an abiding skeleton at the family feast. He has juggled with figures for years to hide the first fraud that he committed when things began to go wrong with him financially in the business of which he is the chief. Securities intrusted to him have been disposed of, but the payment of the interest regularly has lulled suspicion.

But now the crisis is at hand. Unless to-morrow he can get a large sum of money placed to his credit he will have to throw up the sponge and acknowledge that in the fight with Fate he has been beaten at last.

He has worn the mask for years in Society. It would not do for him to drop it and appear anxious and careworn.

But if the worst should happen, and he finds it advisable to start hurriedly for Spain to-morrow night, you will see a very different face under the travelling-cap drawn down over the eyes of the philanthropist as he paces the deck of the Dover to Calais packet.

It is her ladyship's reception, and the beautiful rooms in the family mansion are crowded with brave men and lovely women.

One of the most beautiful of all the beautiful women present stands wreathed in smiles, the centre of a little group of admirers.

Her husband is not at the reception. He very rarely accompanies her. He does not care for the gaieties of Society. One or two of the little group ask about him casually, and the bright, happy wife tells them smilingly, in the slang of the day, that he is "awfully fit," but absorbed in one of his agriculture schemes.

To the eyes that look upon her smiling face that beautiful Society dame is one of the happiest wives in the world. As a matter of fact she has not seen her husband for six months. He went away "by agreement" to one of his seats in the country, leaving her in the town house. That afternoon she received the document which informed her that an action for divorce had been entered against her. In due course the paragraphs will appear in the newspapers, and another Society scandal will be the talk of the town.

The social mask to-day is an adjunct of civilization. The mystery is as to who is wearing it and who is not.

CHAPTER XX.
THE SINS OF THE FATHERS

The children never know—A reprieve at the last moment—A chapter from a life drama—When father comes home from prison—Living down a notorious name

IN the whirl of the world's news, the hurricane of happenings, the rush of events, the impression made upon the public mind by the dramas and tragedies of everyday life is bound to be transient.

All England may be thrilled on Monday by a horror that causes the Press to bristle with headlines, but after the Sunday papers have reproduced the details—perhaps with portraits by way of illustration—the horror loses its grip on the public imagination. A dozen new sensations have come to the front and forced the old one into the background.

There is always a large section of the public that retains its interest in a condemned murderer or murderess right up to the morning of execution. In the years when exciting news was scarcer, "hanging mornings" were quite national events. Special editions of the morning papers came out at ten o'clock with a full account of the painful proceedings, and the last dying speech and confession, if any, of the condemned. The halfpenny evening papers were rushed out at the same time, and the sale was huge. Not long since two halfpenny evening papers quarrelled about their statistics of circulation, and one reproached the other with quoting the figures of its "hanging editions" as those of its everyday sale.

With the execution chapter the story of a murderer ends so far as the general reader is concerned. The interest has been keenly maintained through all the chapters that have gone before relating to the crime, the arrest, the police-court proceedings, the trial, the verdict, scenes in the condemned cell, and, perhaps, the efforts made to obtain a reprieve have kept the story at a high level of interest. But with the last scene of all the details cease to be lovingly dwelt upon in the Press. The curtain falls with the disappearance of the central figure into the pit below the scaffold. The drama is considered—from the point of view of public interest—to be at an end.

Many sympathetic people, especially women, give a passing thought on the day of doom to the innocent relatives of the men and women whose throat the hands of Justice have clutched in the death grip; but the sun rises on another morn, and the tragedy and all concerned in it are lost in the mists of yesterday.

What becomes of the family of a murderer or murderess, of the women and children, the husbands and wives, the brothers and sisters, who bear the name that is branded with infamy for evermore?

Long before the fatal bolt has been withdrawn the children of criminals of fair or good position have disappeared from their old surroundings. They could not stay in their home or walk abroad in the neighbourhood in which they are known. Imagine a group of little ones in the park with their nurse, and a hundred eyes turned upon them pityingly as the children of a man or a woman lying under sentence of death.

The situation, of course, is too terrible to be risked. So from the hour that the tragedy of a great crime becomes public, the near relatives of the criminal try in every way to avoid being identified with it. If they can afford it, they seek a new home, and often arrange to live the remainder of their lives under another name. It happens sometimes that children grow up to manhood and womanhood ignorant of the fact that the name they bear is an assumed one. The ghastly thing that made their own a brand of shame beyond the bearing has mercifully been kept from them.

Even among the poor, when the shadow of the gallows has fallen across the little home, there is an effort to escape from that shadow and all that it means. It is not often that the children remain in the house of tragedy or the street where all their little playmates know their story.

Yet it happens sometimes. Last Christmas morning, wandering in the East End, I entered a house in a little side street packed with a people speaking an alien tongue.

On the staircase a little boy of five and his baby sister of three were playing. Some one had given them a penny box of toys, and they were setting the things out on the stairs.

Not six months previously the body of a murdered woman lay on these stairs. It was there that her husband killed her. The man was hanged. The man was the father, the murdered woman was the mother of the children whom I saw playing last Christmas day on the stairs that had been stained with their mother's blood.

To a boarding-school in the north-west of London there came one day a lady dressed in deep mourning. With evident hesitation she told the head mistress that she wanted to place her two little girls at the school, as she had been ordered to a Continental *Bad* to undergo a course of treatment.

"But before I send my little girls," said the lady, "I shall have to reveal something to you which I must ask you to regard as in the strictest confidence."

Then the unhappy lady, nervous and ill at ease, stammered out her story. She was the widow of a man who had committed suicide at the very moment he was about to be arrested for a murder which was one of the most sensational cases of recent years.

The two children she wished to place at the boarding-school were this man's daughters. The name she and her children bore was a false one. Would the school-mistress, knowing the facts, take the children? The lady felt it would not be right to send them without letting the mistress know the truth.

The head mistress was greatly affected by the tears and the evident distress of her visitor, and when she had satisfied herself on certain points she took the little girls, who knew nothing of the tragedy, and did her best to make them happy in their new surroundings.

If you watch the young ladies of Miss ——————'s well-known boarding-school in the big garden attached to the house, you will see two pretty, fair-haired girls playing gaily with their companions, and you will hear their childish laughter ring out again and again.

The pretty little fair-haired girls are the daughters of the murderer who committed suicide to avoid arrest.

On the bright autumn day that their mother was sentenced to death, three children dressed in deep mourning sat in the sunshine with their governess. They knew that their papa was dead, and that was why they were in black. They were told that their mamma was very, very ill—too ill for her children to be with her—and that she "might die." But the little ones had not the slightest idea that the mother who "might die" was accused of having killed their father. When the verdict had been given, and the sentence pronounced, the children were taken away by a relative and brought up under another name. The law did not in this instance "take its course." At the last moment there was a reprieve, and the death sentence was commuted to one of penal servitude for life.

A curious circumstance has stamped the day of that reprieve on my memory.

On the morning that the Home Secretary's decision was announced I was at Madame Tussaud's Exhibition. The effigy of the condemned woman had, in deference to public opinion, which was divided, been put in a separate room, instead of in the Chamber of Horrors—the usual department for condemned criminals.

On the day of the reprieve a number of people were standing in front of the figure, which was naturally a special attraction. "Ah!" said a man standing near me, "they'll have to take her out of this place altogether some day."

Fifteen years later this woman was released on license, or, as those who cling to old forms of expression say, "ticket-of-leave." That very day her effigy was removed from the premises, and it no longer forms part of the exhibition.

This convict came out into the world. The fact was duly recorded in the Press with considerable emotional comment, and the old dispute as to her guilt or innocence was temporarily revived.

But to how many people did the most dramatic feature of the tragedy present itself? Few of those who re-discussed the celebrated case in all its points remembered that the children of the "murderess" had lived their lives and grown up in ignorance of their mother's fate.

When the unhappy woman was free once more, did she seek her children and reveal herself, or did she mercifully leave their lives unshadowed by the knowledge that the celebrated convict about whose release all the world was talking was their mother?

That is a matter with which the public has no concern, and one into which the Press has very rightly made no attempt to pry. But if the truth were not revealed, if the unhappy mother denied herself the supreme reward of the long years of patient endurance in the silent world, it may have happened that the young people one day as they walked abroad saw a lady looking at them with strange, pathetic intentness, and passed on their way little dreaming that the sad-looking lady was their mother, who had been condemned to death as a murderess long years ago, and had yet lived to see her children grown-up and happy.

No dramatist has given us a situation more intensely human and pathetic than that.

Without the sensational surroundings, strange meetings and reunions are constantly taking place in this great soul-absorbing London of ours. It is a feature of the human drama that is most completely ignored, one that is rarely dwelt upon even by the writers who probe deep down into the mysteries of life in the great City. But the fathers and mothers come home from the prisons and the convict gaols to those who love them.

In the class where no effort is made to conceal the nature of the family misfortune from kinsfolk or neighbours, the absence of the wife and mother is often sympathetically alluded to, and there is joy in the household—a criminal household, possibly—when mother, having paid the penalty of acquiring property without payment, comes back to get father's tea ready and put the children to bed.

Mr. Holmes, the veteran police-court missionary, made the other day what was described as the "startling" statement that he had found some most lovable characters among the wickedest people.

But the confession did not startle those who are in constant touch with the criminal and the vicious.

Society visits the sins of the fathers upon the children, but in the slums and alleys where the criminals congregate the child left temporarily motherless by the action of the law is "everybody's baby."

The poor woman, whose position with regard to children is very much like that of the old lady who resided in a shoe, will take in the child of the woman sent to prison and house it with her own brood, tend it, and feed it.

The home-coming of father, who has done a "length" or a "stretch," is sometimes quite a local event. I went into a little Hoxton house the other day and found great preparations in progress. The eldest girl was scrubbing the floor, the younger children were helping to tidy up. Mother had been out marketing, and on the fire was a saucepan giving forth a savoury smell. The little family seemed so excitedly happy that I ventured to ask the cause of the jubilant bustling.

"Father's coming out of prison to-day," said a little girl, smiling sweetly.

I did not like to ask to be permitted to stay and witness the home-coming of the gentleman, who had frequently returned to the bosom of his family under similar circumstances, but I knew exactly what would happen. The little domestic reunion would be delightful, and all would go well till evening. Then the welcome would be of a more public character, and the hero of the occasion would have considerably more drink offered him than was wise after a long period of enforced abstinence.

Here the home-coming is shorn of its pathos, for it takes place among a class who are openly at war with Society. The criminal's welcome to his home is that of a released prisoner of war—one who fell into the hands of the enemy and is now set free.

The painful home-coming is that of the amateur criminal—the man or woman who has taken a fatal step and endured the *shame* of imprisonment. Then the return of the father or the son to the home to which he has been a stranger so long is often a poignant little domestic drama. I have seen a decent man come out of prison—a man who was innocent, and whom I knew to be innocent—and even in his case the first meeting with friends and acquaintances was a painful trial.

In the respectable family the joy of a relative's return is damped by the knowledge that the prison taint clings, that nothing ever wholly removes it. The man from gaol—the woman from gaol—may be loyally determined never again to deviate by a hair's-breadth from the straight path, but the world does not take the future into consideration when it reckons up the moral worth of a man or woman. The previous conviction is not mentioned in a Court of Justice till the accused has been found guilty. In the world the previous conviction stands against a man throughout his life, though he may never sin again.

That is the burthen that the discharged prisoner of the better class brings with him into the home where his dear ones are waiting to welcome him. He has come back with his shame upon him, and in the shadow of that shame those who bear his name will have to live.

It is to escape the shame that a new name, a new environment, sometimes a new sky, is sought. Far away from the land of their birth there are to-day hundreds of families expatriated by the sin of one member of it. In the Continental cities there are to be met with Englishmen and Englishwomen with whose doings at one time all England rang. They have come abroad, sometimes to hide themselves, but frequently that their children may be educated in Continental schools where the name they bear will carry no scandal with it to the ears of their classmates.

Hidden away under assumed names there are tragedies which at one time have been the talk of the town. The stage affords greater facilities for a sudden change of identity than any other profession, and for that reason many young men and women who have a desire to be known by a new name do their best to get on to it as a means of livelihood.

In commercial life, before a young man or a young woman can secure an appointment of any kind a reference must be given, and the giving necessitates the revelation of the real name, and probably the family story the applicant is most anxious to conceal.

But for the chorus of a musical comedy, for a small part in a play on tour, the applicant can give any name he or she may choose. There are no such things as references. All that the manager wants is appearance, voice, and the possession of a certain amount of ability.

There happened once in the rehearsals of a drama of mine an incident far more dramatic than any I had put in the piece itself.

One of the scenes was laid in Millbank, in those days a gaol for female convicts. Anxious to have the details correct, I invited a friend of mine who had held a high official position in the gaol to come to the dress rehearsal. He sat by me in the stalls. When the curtain rose on the prison scene a number of female convicts were standing on the stage in charge of a warderess.

My friend eyed them critically to see that the dress was worn correctly and the cap put on properly. At one of the convicts he gazed intently. When he had passed the scene as correct in detail he turned to me and said—

"I couldn't help staring at that young lady—the fourth in the row. She is the living image of a woman who was in my charge ten years ago—Mrs. ———— ————; you remember the case?"

I did remember it. Mrs. ———————— was a lady for whom there was considerable sympathy. Maddened by her husband's neglect and ill-treatment, she shot him with a revolver one night after a fierce quarrel. The wound was nearly fatal, and the unfortunate woman was awarded a term of penal servitude. "I never saw such an extraordinary resemblance to Mrs. ———————— in her convict dress," said the official; "but, of course, it is a coincidence. Mrs. ———————— was old enough to be this young lady's mother."

After the act was over I went behind the scenes to make a few alterations, and I told the young actress "convict" that the gentleman in front was a prison official, and I added jokingly, "He says you are the living image of Mrs. ————————, who was at Millbank for the attempted murder of her husband."

I expected the young lady to laugh, but, to my astonishment, the colour faded from her face and she became visibly distressed.

"What a dreadful idea!" she gasped. "It frightens me—I—I wish you hadn't told me."

She walked quickly away, and I thought no more of the incident. Long afterwards I learnt the truth.

The young actress who had attracted the attention of the prison official *was* the daughter of Mrs. ————————. Under another name she had gone upon the stage. It was a strange coincidence that the daughter of a female convict should be called upon to represent a female convict in Millbank before an official who had been at Millbank when her mother was there.

CHAPTER XXI.
THE ROMANCE OF REALITY

She waits in vain—Messengers from the First Cousin of the Moon— Witches and wise women—The seventh child of a seventh child— Secret societies of vengeance—Italy in London

THE strange, the weird, the romantic, may be found at every turn of the great maze of mystery which is called London.

The homes of mystery and romance lie often at our very doors, unknown and unexpected. We pass a scene that the novelist or the dramatist could turn to thrilling account, and to us it suggests not even a passing thought of wonder.

Here is a house in a fashionable road in that part of the north-west which borders on Hampstead.

It is an ordinary villa residence. There are flowers in the windows, and all the signs of well-to-do occupation. But in this ordinary-looking villa there is a room at the back in which the light of day never penetrates. The shutters are always closed, the door is always kept locked. Only one person has that key, the lady to whom the house belongs. She lives there with a brother and a sister, who came to make their home with her in her hour of distress, and who do their best to brighten a life that has known a great sorrow.

The lady came to the house a young married woman. It was the house that she and her fiancé selected and furnished to be their home when they returned from their honeymoon.

The young couple knew in it one happy month. Then the young husband went out one day and never returned. From that hour no inkling of his fate ever reached the unhappy bride, whose reason almost gave way under the strain and stress of the long agony of suspense.

On the day that he went out from the home to which he was never to return, the young husband was expected back at six o'clock in the evening.

It was his birthday, and a little birthday dinner had been arranged, to which a few intimate friends had been invited.

It was the young wife's first dinner-party, and she took great pride in the arrangement of the room and the floral decorations of the table.

The table as it was laid out for that little dinner-party remains to-day. The flowers are dead and withered, the table-linen is yellow with age, the furniture is faded and decayed, and desolation has settled on the scene. But the wife so suddenly and mysteriously widowed refused from the first to allow a thing in the room to be touched. The birthday-table is still laid for the husband, who will never come home again.

Here in the south-west of London is a little old-fashioned shop in which second-hand furniture and curios are sold.

There is nothing out of the common in the shop, yet it has its strange romance. If you look over the doorway you will see a Chinese name. If you enter the shop the young lady who comes forward, though she has Oriental features, addresses you in ordinary English, with perhaps a slightly Cockney twang.

The shop was founded by her father, a young Chinaman who suddenly appeared in London. No one knew where he came from. He wore Chinese dress and a pigtail, and started in business with a hired barrow, with which he went round to houses in the neighbourhood, buying the odds and ends that people wanted to get rid of.

Gradually he became less Chinese in appearance. The pigtail went, and he took to European clothes. He seemed to have prospered, for he took a little shop, and later on married an Englishwoman.

It was quite a humble little shop at first, but there passed in and out of it occasionally Chinamen who were evidently grandees. They came in elegant carriages, and, according to report, they were mandarins.

Once the carriage of the Chinese Ambassador stopped in the street, and the representative of the Brother of the Sun and First Cousin of the Moon passed into the shop and remained for a quarter of an hour in the little back parlour closeted with the Chinaman who had come here from nowhere, and had started business in England buying old bottles, old iron, and old rags.

Every one in the street knew the Chinaman, and gradually many became his tenants, for he bought a good deal of property round about. But no one ever penetrated the mystery of his connection with the great mandarins who from time to time visited him, and no one was ever able to form the faintest idea why the Chinese Ambassador came to interview him in the back parlour.

The Chinese name is over the door, the Chinaman's children are carrying on the business at the present moment. They are in everything but appearance English men and women. The Chinaman himself lies in a London cemetery, where the broken stones are on his grave. But the mystery of who he was, and what interest the high representatives of the great Chinese Emperor had in him, remains unfathomed.

While we are in Chinese company let us cross London to the east and enter the Chinese quarter, which is still round Lime-house Causeway, although many of the lodging-house proprietors and opium-den keepers have moved into High Street, Poplar.

Here is a little shop which looks innocent enough. The only suggestion that it is an opium den is in the odd-looking little pipes exhibited for sale in the window.

You may pass up and down the street all day and not see a soul enter this shop. If you peer in you will see something in Chinese characters over the door that leads to the inner portion of the premises. If you were to enter you would be in the presence of a Joss and the strange worship of the wooden image. Here in the heart of living London are the mysteries of the East to be found—here you may see phases of life as they might have been depicted in some side street of Pekin by Guy Boothby.

To this house opium smokers with strange histories have come again and again. It was here that an English opium smoker, who had been searched for in vain by his friends for many months, was found at last, lost to knowledge of himself, lost to everything except the mad craving for the drug that had degraded him from a high estate to lie cheek by jowl with the strange men of the East, who bring their mysteries with them for awhile to the world's port, and then vanish to be seen no more.

The Londoner may think when he sees high up upon a tapering flagstaff a red lamp glowing in the darkness of the night that it is intended, by the small body of men and women who have imbibed the occultism of the East, to light the wandering Mahatmas home.

Though the general knowledge of the rites of the Theosophists is vague, there is no concealment about the temples of the worshippers. But there are strange rites practised in the heart of busy London, and there is no sign or token given of the meeting-place of those who indulge in them.

In a gloomy synagogue in a by-street of Alien Land the patriarchal Jew may be seen writing out the sacred amulets and scrolls by the light of a guttering candle—a picture for a Rembrandt; but no one but her dupes sees the "witch" or the "wise woman," who still carries on her trade in the twentieth century, making the charms and the love philtres that she knows where to sell.

The West End palmists and fortune-tellers flourished for a time and had their day, and went down before the arm of the law; but a far more dangerous trade than theirs, which did but minister to a foolish, fashionable craze, is still carried on daily and nightly in secret in unsuspected places.

It is nine o'clock at night and the darkness has descended over London. At the top of a street near Victoria Station, once inhabited by the well-to-do, but now fallen into the seediness of floor-letting, a cab stops and a lady closely veiled alights.

She makes her way to one of the houses, looking furtively behind her now and then. She rings the bell and is admitted.

If we follow her we shall see her descend the stairs to the basement. She is shown into a room dimly lighted and fantastically draped, and filled with strange objects.

A dark, sallow-faced woman, clad in a curious Eastern robe, receives her, and the door is closed and locked.

The woman passes for a seeress—a modern witch. She is consulted by women of education, women who come to her to gaze into the crystal and the ink pool, to peer into the future, and who—strange as it may seem to common sense, level-headed people—implicitly believe in the supernatural powers of the wily adventuress, the cunning woman who trades upon their credulity.

We can understand the ignorant servant-girl who pays the half-crown she can ill spare for some wretched hag in a garret to read the cards for her and tell her her future; but there is nothing more amazing in the mysteries of London than the hold which the clairvoyante and the "divineress"—generally, according to themselves, "the seventh child of a seventh child"—still have upon the minds of women of education and position.

There is hardly one of the clairvoyantes who practised in the West until the law stepped in who is not still carrying on the business, though in a more secret and a less profitable manner.

Here is a house that the agents would call "a desirable villa residence." It stands in a long garden at the corner of one of the leafy roads of St. John's Wood.

Within its walls meets a little band of men and women who go through strange ceremonies and perform strange rites, and almost worship as their leader a woman who calls herself a prophetess, and who has persuaded her ignorant dupes that she is directly appointed to save them from death. The semblance of death they will know, but their souls will pass into other bodies, and in a reincarnated state they will continue to live upon the earth in greater happiness and greater health and strength and well-being than they ever knew before.

The policeman on duty passes the house at night and flashes his lantern on the door, but he has no idea of the strange orgies of exaltation which take place behind the closed shutters of that charming villa residence.

There are "offerings" to the prophetess, the giving up of jewellery and "adornments" for the good of the cause, and so it may be that one day the Old Bailey will see "a prophetess" in the dock again, and the spectators will look with astonishment at the men and women who enter the witness-box to tell a story that will startle the newspaper reader and make the humdrum world open its eyes and say, "Can such things be in these days of enlightenment?"

In a road running off the outer circle of Regent's Park there is another house of mystery. It is walled in in front, and there is a door in the wall which is always kept locked.

If you ring the bell a man-servant will open the little trap in the door and look at you keenly.

You are not likely to be admitted unless you have satisfied the janitor that your visit is expected, and that your presence will be welcome to the master of the house.

The master of the house is a foreigner. The name in which he dwells in the house is not his own. He is one of the most trusted agents of the great Revolutionary Party, and his guests are "comrades" who come with messages from the capitals of Europe.

More than one plot which has startled the world has been arranged in that ordinary, unromantic-looking house, and its walls have from time to time sheltered men whose whereabouts certain European Governments were exceedingly anxious to discover.

The Mafia! We read of this terrible Italian secret society and its murderous doings in the land of the stiletto, and we accept the printed stories with a vague suspicion that they belong to modern Italian opera rather than real life.

But the emissaries of the Mafia—the Society of Vengeance—are tracking down their prey in the dull, drab streets of our own prosaic city.

If you pass along the Clerkenwell Road you will come to a side street that dips down into a hollow, and this hollow, though open to the view of all who pass along the bustling London thoroughfare, is perhaps the most un-English spot in the whole of England.

As you pass the top of Eyre Street Hill—that is the opening which leads to the district we call Little Italy—you will see two policemen in uniform standing together. You will see two policemen always there after nightfall, and when there is trouble they go down into the hollow together.

For the natives of Little Italy are given to sudden outbursts of anger, and then the knife flashes and the pistol shot rings out on the air. Occasionally, when the quarrel is an ordinary one, which has arisen over a sweetheart, or perhaps over the wine bottles in the kitchen of the padrone, the English police may make a capture.

But when the knife or the pistol is used to carry out the sentence of the Mafia, the agent of that dreaded society who has executed the "order" with which he was entrusted by the chiefs in Naples, or, perhaps, in Palermo, finds it no difficult matter to lie concealed from the most active search the English officers of justice may make.

The ordinary assassin may be denounced and given up by neighbours who were witnesses of the outrage, but the man of the Mafia is not likely to be betrayed by an Italian who wants to continue in the peaceable enjoyment of his life.

It sounds very like a sensational novelette, but it is plain fact. The Mafia agents who stab or shoot in Little Italy are shielded by those who fear to offend the society, and an early opportunity is taken of getting them secretly out of the country. Their mission accomplished, they go back to Italy.

I have spent more than one night in the kitchen of a padrone. I have been into most of the houses from floor to basement, even into the underground cellars, where at night-time they dance the Tarantella, and I have found the inhabitants of Little Italy a hard-working and civil lot of men and women, very much more prosperous, and with a far higher standard of comfort, than we gather from sensational newspaper articles about ice-cream vendors and organ-grinders. But there are two classes of inhabitants, the North Italians and the South Italians, and there is as much difference between them in temperament as there is between a Scotchman and an Irishman.

The Piedmontese, who are in Little Italy in large numbers, are mostly paviors and labourers, and they repudiate the acts of violence for which the district has, or had, a bad name.

If you speak in a lodging-house where the clients are Piedmontese about the stabbings and shootings, they will say, "Oh yes, the Neapolitans, perhaps—but not us."

But both North and South know the Mafia, and would hesitate to speak the truth about any of its members if the truth were likely to do the said members harm. If you were to ask in Little Italy to-morrow about the Mafia, they would even deny that its agents were to be found there at all.

But they *are* there, and on more than one occasion they have made their presence felt in the most approved manner of the vendetta as it finds expression in Italian opera.

In every quarter of London, in the most matter-of-fact environment, the romance of reality is to be found—a romance as thrilling as anything the sensational novelist could invent and give to the world with a certainty that his invention would be looked upon as wildly improbable.

Nothing that is imagined and invented is so astounding as that which really is, and the most astounding thing is that the existence of the reality is unsuspected by the people who live constantly in close proximity to it.

Over much that is strange and terrible in modern Babylon the veil is wisely drawn by those who write for the great public. In Paris there is less discretion, and the sores of the city are laid bare for the idle and the curious to stare at them.

If a writer knowing London wrote with the lack of reticence which distinguishes the Parisian who knows Paris, the result would be one beside which all the "startling revelations" that are imagined and dressed up by fictionists disguised as journalists would pale into insignificance.

CHAPTER XXII.
SOME CONTRASTS

The inquest and the garden party—A policeman sits behind the screen—The portrait of a prosperous impostor—From his wife's death-bed to the House—The judge and his pet dog—Tea and cakes while they wait for the sentence

UNDER the trees in the garden the tables are spread for a pastoral fête. Smiling waitresses are handing ices and claret cup and strawberries and cream to daintily-gowned ladies who are sitting in the shade and chatting gaily with their admiring cavaliers. I come out from a little building in the grounds and gaze at the fair and festive scene. As I see the pretty frocks and pretty faces, and listen to the rippling laughter, I cannot help being struck by the vivid contrast between the tragedy I have that moment left and the comedy I have come upon.

These grounds are the grounds of a famous hospital, and the company are gathered together under the trees after listening to speeches and witnessing the presentation of prizes in the great hall of the institution.

I come through the little door of the out-building to step right into the joy of life, and the door as it closes behind has shut away a tragedy. Behind it lies a dead man upon whom the verdict of a coroner's jury has been pronounced.

I am not easily upset, and I have looked in my professional wanderings upon many gruesome sights, but my nerves have been sorely tried during the five minutes I have been inside that little out-building of a great hospital.

There were only two men inside it when I entered, and one of them was dead. The living man was the inquest porter, and he was spending the blazing summer afternoon in giving back to the dead one the shape and impress of humanity.

It was a sight to make the unaccustomed spectator shudder, and I only lingered long enough to hear the story of the tragedy. Then I passed out again into the sunshine and found myself at a garden party. I looked at the charming scene and the smiling faces of the fair guests; I listened to the rippling laughter and the musical clink of the ice in the cooling wine cups, and I could not help thinking of the strangeness of the contrast. Only a few inches of space and a wooden door separated the garden party from the dead-house.

Not one fair visitor in that gay crowd had the faintest idea of what was happening within a few yards of where she sat in the sunshine under the trees eating strawberries and cream.

As I passed the group a young lady whom I knew came towards me. "What a delightful place this is!" she said. "Really, I never thought a hospital was so charming."

"Charming" seemed a strange word to apply to a hospital. But in our great palaces of pain to-day the eye is constantly cheered, and in the note of colour and comfort the casual visitor forgets the anguish that lies hidden beneath the gay coverlets and behind the pretty curtains.

Here is a hospital ward that an artist might delight in. The colour scheme is soothing to the eye. Along the ward are little tables on which stand bowls and vases of daintily arranged flowers. In the centre of the ward is a square of carpet of a soft artistic green. A young lady with a basket of roses is passing from bed to bed. She places one of her sweet flowers in the hand of every sufferer.

Outside the sun is shining and the birds are singing. The scene is delightful, and the visitor forgets the pain of the patients in the charm of the environment.

But at the far end of the room there is a screen. Behind that screen is a bed on which lies a man white and motionless, with his throat swathed in surgical bandages.

Beside the bed, hidden also by the screen, sits a policeman.

The visitor sees the flowers and the pretty coverlets and curtains, the polished floors, and the soft green art carpet. But he does not see the horror behind the screen; he does not suspect it, for he is not allowed to go near enough to know that the screen conceals anything at all.

The man behind the screen was brought to the hospital with a gaping wound in his throat. He had inflicted it himself, after stabbing the wife who lay by his side. The woman may die. She is in another part of the hospital. When the man is well enough he will be taken to prison. If the woman dies the charge against him will be murder. Night and day in that charmingly arranged, flower-decorated ward, the officer of justice sits guarding, not a patient, but a prisoner.

In the next bed lies a young man who is rapidly approaching convalescence. His happy wife bends over him with tender love in her eyes. The sunshine of returning life and the shadow of a dreadful death are separated only by a few inches of polished floor and a little table on which stands a bowl of roses.

The world once rang with the story of the Tichborne Claimant. The romance of that colossal imposture will be told again and again for many a long year to come.

In the days when he was still "Sir Roger" to the great public, I met the Claimant and conversed with him. Long after the huge edifice of fraud had crumbled to the dust I made the acquaintance of some members of the Orton family, and from them received certain photographs, which I added to my souvenirs of famous cases.

After he had served his sentence the Claimant made a confession, which he sent to a weekly newspaper. Later on he tried to withdraw the confession, but it was substantially true, and its publication destroyed the last vestige of faith which some few people still had in him.

After this "Sir Roger" gradually dropped out of public knowledge. He lived quietly and meanly in furnished rooms in a street in Marylebone. In these rooms he died. He was taken to the Marylebone mortuary, and there one sunny morning I went to see him in his coffin.

A gravel path bordered by flowers and trees leads to the hostel of the dead. After I had seen the Claimant, the adventurous life ended at last, the lying lips closed for ever in the eternal silence, I came back along that flower-bordered pathway and out into the busy thoroughfare.

My way home lay through a long street of private houses. Passing one of the houses, I looked up at the windows of the drawing-room floor, and the thought of the dead man I had left came vividly back to me. For in these rooms there lived for many years a gentleman whose name was on every one's lips in the days of the great Tichborne trial. He believed in the Claimant implicitly. He found large sums of money for "Sir Roger" during the years that the case remained undecided.

Long after the butcher of Wapping had gone to reduce his weight on a convict regime, his friend and supporter took this house. He lived there and died there, and up to the day of his death, quaint and eccentric in many things, he still believed that Arthur Orton was Sir Roger Tichborne, Bart., of the B.K.

There were many mementoes of the old Tichborne days in the possession of his former supporter. When he died he left them to his housekeeper. His housekeeper kept the house on, and let a portion of it in apartment. I knew, for I had seen them, that the Tichborne relics were still in the drawing-room. One of them was a portrait of the Claimant, taken in the days of his prosperity, when the Tichborne Bonds had been put on the market and money was pouring in. I could not resist the temptation of calling and telling the lady of the house of the Claimant's death, and asking to see the portraits and the relics. There they stood as I remembered them in the old days. The portrait of "Sir Roger" was on the old-fashioned chiffonier, standing between two little vases of flowers. I looked at the smiling face of the prosperous impostor in his heyday a few minutes after I had seen Arthur Orton lying in the parish mortuary.

A nurse from one of the big nursing institutions has been sent for hurriedly to a woman who is lying dangerously ill in cheap apartments in Pimlico.

Nurses are accustomed to contrasts. One week they may be tending a patient in a magnificent mansion, the next they may be in charge of a case where the surroundings are of the humblest description.

The nurse whose adventure I am about to tell did not particularly like the look of the house to which she had been summoned. Her quick, professional eye read the character of the inmates before she had passed through the hall into the room occupied by her patient.

The patient, a woman of about five-and-thirty, was what is technically known as "a drink case." The doctor who had been in attendance and telephoned to the institution was in the room waiting for the nurse.

"She is very bad," he said, "and I don't think there is much hope. I have ascertained who she is, and I have communicated with her husband. He may come this afternoon or this evening."

At eight o'clock in the evening a gentleman called and asked to see Mrs. —————————. He saw the nurse and told her the doctor had informed him that Mrs. ————————— was ill. He asked to see her alone.

The visitor, a man of about fifty, remained alone with the sick woman for a few minutes. Then he came out and spoke to the nurse.

"She is very bad," he said. "Does the doctor give any hope?"

The nurse shook her head. "Very little," she replied.

Two days afterwards the blinds were down in the Pimlico lodging-house. The patient was dead.

The morning after the visitor had called, the nurse read the daily paper, and, because a certain fact which had come to her knowledge had aroused her curiosity, she turned to the Parliamentary Report.

A well-known and distinguished member of Parliament had made a speech the previous evening which had attracted general attention, and which was reproduced in full, as it was on a burning question of the day.

The politician had gone from the bed of the dying woman in the Pimlico lodging-house to the House of Commons to make the speech of the evening. The woman whom he had called to see he had not spoken to for many years. But she was his wife. The dying woman had revealed her identity to the doctor, and had implored him to let her husband know of her whereabouts and to beg him to come and see her.

In his Memoirs Lord Brampton, known to an earlier generation as Sir Henry Hawkins, quotes a little article written about his famous dog Jack, and says he wishes he knew who the author was.

I have not written to Lord Brampton telling him that the words he quotes are mine. If I refer to them here, it is because the great judge's pet was always associated in my mind with a vivid contrast.

Many years ago I was in a provincial town where a man was being tried for murder. I went to the court and heard the trial, and was present when the prisoner was sentenced to death. I saw the judge upon the Bench with the black cap upon his head, and I heard him pronounce the awful words of doom.

Early the next morning I went for a walk to a rural suburb of the town. Crossing a meadow I came upon a gentleman who was also taking a country stroll. In the middle of the meadow he was playing with his dog. He had a piece of stick in his hand, and the dog was jumping up and barking, and eagerly demanding in canine language that the stick should be thrown.

The smiling gentleman romping with his dog in the morning sunshine was the stem judge who had the previous evening sentenced a man to death. I recognized the dog before I recognized his master, because I had met Jack at Worcester Assizes, and had seen him held on a lead by his master, solemnly escorted by the javelin men, who met the Judge at Worcester Station to accompany him to his lodgings.

I can imagine no greater contrast than that between the solemn procession illustrating the majesty of the law and the antics in which Jack indulged as he followed the javelin men. The contrast is hardly a London one, but it is permissible to mention it here, as Jack, the famous judge's dog, was a great London celebrity as well as a provincial one.

A fashionable London church is filled with flowers and palms. The pews are crowded with pretty women and handsome men. Outside the church there is an eager, expectant crowd that is with difficulty kept back from the red carpet under the awning.

The bridesmaids have arrived and are waiting in the porch. Presently a carriage drives up, and there is a buzz of admiration as the beautiful and aristocratic bride alights, and, leaning on the arm of her father, enters the church.

There is a bishop at the altar, and he is "assisted" by a distant relative of the bridegroom. The service is fully choral, and the lady journalists are taking notes of the dresses for tomorrow's newspapers.

As the bridal party comes out of the church there is a little accident. A man falls in a fit in the crowd, and the policeman, turning to help him, the people surge up, and the bridal procession is interrupted. In the confusion some of the flowers in the bride's bouquet become detached and fall to the ground. A workman with a sad, careworn face bends down and picks them up. He will take them home when his work is over. The flowers of the bride's bouquet will lie on the breast of the dead girl who has given him a year of happy wedded life, and now lies dead in the desolate little home.

The fair young bride of the West will know nothing of the dead wife in the East. But the flowers that were bought for the bridal of the one will lie in the coffin of the other.

******

Of all the dramatic contrasts of our modern London life few are so striking as those which are conventional at a trial for murder at the Old Bailey.

In the shadow of death on the last day of the trial sits the prisoner, while a large portion of the spectators take the proceedings as an interesting and sometimes thrilling form of entertainment.

There are rooms set apart in the Old Bailey for the necessary refreshment of officials connected with the court, and in one of these, while the jury are deliberating on their verdict, and the prisoner is waiting in the cells below in feverish agony, lady visitors take tea and cakes, and male visitors have coffee and cigarettes.

In the corridors of the court there are little groups chatting together, and the talk is not always of the trial.

On the emotional man surveying the scene and listening to the light conversation, sometimes to the jokes, this feature of a murder trial makes a vivid impression. He looks around him at the light-hearted groups and thinks of the dumb despair of the man or woman who waits, white-faced and terror-stricken, in a cell below the dock.

And when with the solemn words of the death sentence ringing in his ears he passes out of the court into the street, and the newsboys rush by him shouting "All the winners," the contrast is complete.

One evening, in a quiet side street in the south of London, there floated through an open window the sound of a banjo. Near the window sat a man. He was amusing himself with the banjo, and presently he played a cake-walk tune. The children in the street heard the music and began to dance to it, and the man played on.

An hour or two later he gave himself up at the police-station. He had murdered his little girl "to save her from her mother," he stated at his trial. The child was lying dead in the room while he played the banjo and the merry children danced the cake-walk in the roadway below.

Not long ago, on a bitter winter day, I passed along the Euston Road. Outside the soup kitchen stood a shivering crowd of penniless men and women.

Up the street in front of me went a tall, military-looking man walking with a beautifully dressed woman.

Opposite the soup kitchen the pair stopped for a moment and looked at the pitiful spectacle. Suddenly the woman gave a little cry of distress.

"Oh! come along," she exclaimed—"Jack's there."

They passed rapidly along, and I stayed and watched the poor wretches shivering in the blizzard, and waiting for the food that charity had made possible for them.

Presently I saw the military man come back. He crossed the road, and, going up to a man of about forty—refined-looking even in his rags—he slipped a sovereign into his hand and then walked rapidly away.

The well-dressed man was an officer in the Army. He was engaged to the lady with whom he was walking. The ragged outcast waiting at the soup kitchen was the lady's husband, from whom she had been divorced some years previously.

She was an actress well known in musical comedy. Some little time ago she left the stage, and her marriage with Captain ——————— was announced. When I saw the announcement I remembered the soup kitchen in the Euston Road and the ragged outcast to whom his wife sent a sovereign by the man she was about to marry.

The contrasts of life in the great city meet us at every turn. Those that are sharply defined—the wealth and the poverty, the happiness and the misery—we look upon and understand; but the greatest contrasts of all are those which fail to appeal to us because we cannot see beneath the surface of things as they are.

CHAPTER XXIII.
AT DEAD OF NIGHT

Flotsam and Jetsam—The midnight coffee-stall—A sense of "life going on"—A long row of three-storey houses—Sleeping on a staircase—The burglar's business hours

FROM the moment that Big Ben booms the hour of midnight over the great City the sounds of its ceaseless life begin to diminish in volume.

Silence comes to her never, but over vast spaces between the midnight and the dawn there reign a peace and a quietude unfamiliar to the ears of day.

But even in the shadows and silent places lurk the mysteries of humanity. The lords of life and death look down upon a drama that is played. The sentinel stars keep watch over a battlefield strewn with the victims of the human conflict.

The palatial hostelries of wealth that glow with lights far into the night are divided but by a few yards from the silent river, on which gleam here and there the dull red lamps of black barges and vessels moored at the wharves or anchored in the stream.

But between the gilded guest-houses of the wealthy and the river freighted with the world's wealth there lie scattered heaps of human wreckage.

Walk along the Embankment in the dead of night, and you will see the outcasts lying huddled together in corners of the stonework, sometimes reaching in lines of misery almost to the last step by the water's edge.

Every seat is occupied by homeless men and women, tramps and tatterdemalions of both sexes, who are camping out because they have not the money for a bed, and prefer the canopy of heaven to the ceiling of the refuge or the casual ward.

Every now and then a policeman passes, creeping along in silent shoes that give no warning of his approach, and as he flashes his lantern on the faces of the sleepers you can see that they are young and old and middle-aged men and women who have gone under, and men and women who were born under and never tried to rise.

There is no mystery about the bulk of them, but now and again amid the herd of hapless ones you will find traces of refinement and intelligence; the look of despair may be in the sunken eyes raised to yours from a row of brutal and sinister faces.

From one of these dormitories of the desolate a woman rose wearily one night as the dawn was breaking, and, climbing the parapet, dropped into the river.

She was rescued and charged with attempting to commit suicide. The magistrate, struck by the refinement of the poor creature's voice and manner, asked the police-court missionary to see her.

To the missionary the homeless, penniless woman who had staggered in the dawn from a seat on the Embankment to end her misery in the merciful river confided her story. He took her to his own home and sought her friends. They had not seen her for years, and were ignorant of her fate. Her story was as old as the first love tragedy—a woman's faith and a man's treachery, and then the shame that hides itself away from all who knew and cared.

The outcast of the Embankment who leapt to a suicide's grave has taken her old place in her father's home, and the past is forgotten. That home is across the Atlantic. Not long ago her people came to London, and she came with them, travelling with all the comfort and luxury of wealth.

From the window of her room in one of the great hotels she may have looked out in the hush of the starlit night at the crouching outcasts of whom she once was one.

Through the long night, in deserted streets and squares, the human shadows pass, some creeping furtively as if ashamed, others fierce and reckless prowlers of the darkness, waiting for prey.

Along the main thoroughfares of London, from the West to the East, from the North to the South, there is never the intense loneliness of the streets that lie off the track. There the late Londoner and early Londoner divide the night between them, and as the late brougham or cab bears the tired pleasure-seeker home to rest, the carts and the wagons begin to wend their way to the markets and the docks and the great railway stations.

Here and there along the line of route there are belated groups of men gathered at the night coffee-stalls. The last reveller has hardly slunk sleepily home before the early workers begin to make their way into the streets.

But at the dead of night in many a big thoroughfare, crowded and busy in the daytime, there is a sense of loneliness and mystery.

It is past two o'clock in the morning, and a young woman, who has perhaps returned from her late work at the West, stops for a moment outside a popular theatre in a main street in the East End of London. There is no one on the broad pavement but herself. A little way off across the road is a coffee-stall. It is deserted, and the keeper is dozing in his box.

Two young men come lounging up the street. One of them knows the girl and greets her by name, and in a friendly way invites her to have a cup of coffee.

The two men and the girl linger for a few moments at the stall, and the girl says good night and goes towards her home. The young men pass along the street and disappear. No one sees them again until six o'clock in the morning, when a boy and a man notice them coming out of a closed shop.

In the dead of night these two young men disappeared. No one met them, no one saw them. When the time came to trace their movements, only the girl who stood outside the theatre at two o'clock, and a young man who passed them a little earlier, could be found to give Justice the information she sought. For Justice laid her hand upon the men and charged them with being concerned in a crime for which they eventually paid the penalty on the gallows.

It is in the dead of night, when London sleeps, that crime stalks abroad warily and plies its trade. The policeman passes on his beat, but the darkness hides the figures that creep along the streets or crouch behind high walls, and, defying bolts and bars, enter the houses of the rich—uninvited guests.

Having secured any valuables they can lay their hands on, they steal away stealthily to their lairs, and buy a paper the next day to read about the daring burglary which has been discovered by the early maidservant as she goes yawning down the stairs to light the kitchen fire.

The darkness of the night is the burglar's hour, for then he knows that the better parts of residential London are silent as the grave. And yet in the deadest hour of night a mighty crowd can be gathered as if by magic in a few minutes.

There is a red glow in the sky, the cry of "Fire!" rings out, and the engine rattles past with the thrilling shouts of the men, and instantly sleeping London wakes and pours a half-dressed crowd of men and women into the streets. A city of the dead becomes a city of wild, turbulent life in an instant.

There is no mystery of the City greater than that sudden gathering of vast crowds in the dead of night to see someone else's house on fire. In some areas the news spreads from street to street, even at such an hour, so rapidly that a huge mob is crowding every approach to the burning building before any of the fire-engines have been able to reach the scene.

In the neighbourhood of the great stations where the mail trains arrive between three and four o'clock in the morning, there is a sense of "life going on" that attracts a certain kind of loafer—a nondescript lounger totally different from the back-against-the-wall specimen of the daytime.

If some of those people who are attracted to centres of movement during the small hours could be tracked to their homes, we should be astonished to find that a good many of them are in respectable circumstances. They are generally men living alone, either bachelors or widowers, and some of them are professional men and the victims of insomnia.

There are men who get up constantly in the middle of the night and go out "to get rid of their thoughts," as one of the victims of this peculiar form of distraction once told me. These men haunt the streets in the dead of night; but they do not choose the lonely places, they want to see their fellow-men who are still awake and about, and the railway station with its bustle in the middle of the night has a peculiar attraction for them.

They wait about on the platform, most of them, as if they were going to meet friends; they watch the cabs away until the last luggage-laden four-wheeler has crawled out of the station, and then when the lights are turned down they go slowly out into the street again to make their own way home.

There is one phase of London at the dead of night which is remarkable, but it is not advisable to investigate it if you are alone. To see it you must spend an hour or two in "the streets with the open doors," and these streets are not to be recommended to the stranger between the hours of I and 4 a.m.

Picture to yourself a long row of three-storey houses, grimy, monotonous, dilapidated. There is not one house that has not broken window-panes, either stuffed with rag or pasted across with newspaper. The stucco has peeled away in many places. Where it is left it is black with grime.

To each of these houses there is a front door. But it has no knocker, and by the side of it are no bells. Passed through the hole in the door, intended originally for a key, there is a short piece of cord or string. The string is there that the inmates may, if so minded, open or pull the door to after them.

These doors are never bolted or locked. If they were the tenants would be seriously inconvenienced, because they come in at all hours of the night, and pass up the broken, dilapidated stairways to their rooms.

If you waited at the end of the street through the small hours you would occasionally see rough-looking men come slouching along on their way home. When one of these men reaches the door of his residence he either pushes it open with his hand or his shoulder, or, if he is not in an amiable mood, he probably kicks it open.

Anyone may pull the doors open in such a street and enter, and the consequence is that occasionally a tenant has to pick his way up the stairs over the reclining forms of travellers who have taken up their quarters for the night without any preliminary negotiations with the landlord. These people are of the same class as those who make a dormitory of the Embankment, the seats on the bridges and in the public thoroughfares and Trafalgar Square, and in the mews and stable-yards, and under railway arches.

In fine weather they may sleep in the streets, in bad weather they make themselves comfortable on the stairways of low-class tenant "blocks" and the houses with "the doors that are always open." They used to be called "'Appy Dossers"—a term the late Lord Salisbury with a smile asked me to explain when I used it in giving evidence before the Royal Commission on the Housing of the Working Classes.

Sometimes these people have a room for a week or two, then they put in a week at the 'appy dosser business. That is why the tenants step over them with a certain amount of consideration. They themselves, though they have a room in the house this week for which they are paying rent, may be glad next week to sleep on the stairs for nothing.

At the Old Bailey, when the Strattons were tried for the Mask murder, one of the women was asked where she slept when they were turned out of their lodgings. "On a staircase," was the reply.

But there is a certain etiquette even among the 'appy dossers. It is not considered good manners to settle down for the night on somebody else's staircase until after one o'clock, and the usual hour for rising is between five and six.

In the dead of night strange burthens are borne across the sleeping city. It is in the early morning that the night watchman, quitting his post in some great works or storeyard, generally makes the gruesome discovery which is to fill the Press for many days with the "mystery" that all classes of readers delight in.

Skulking through the silent, deserted streets go men at war with society, men living by crime, who under the cover of darkness ply their perilous trade, ready armed to kill if need be, either the sleeping householder or the guardian of the night who interrupts them at their villainous work.

Sometimes they have accomplished their task and are returning to their homes with the spoil upon them, but so cunningly concealed that they can pass the policeman strolling on his lonely beat without exciting his suspicion.

For these men—the professional burglars who follow crime as a craft—plan and plot beforehand with the strategical skill of a general arranging an attack upon the enemy. After they have studied the "crib" they intend to "crack," and ascertained the habits of its inmates, they frequently walk the route they intend to follow once or twice beforehand in the night, noting everything by the way.

If you study the details of famous burglaries that have been brought home to their authors, you will find that the men concerned have made elaborate calculations, not only of the means of access, but of the position of the moon—the "Oliver" of the highwayman of the days of the romance of the road. "Shall we do it to-night?" is frequently the question asked when the accomplices meet to confer. They know what they mean to do, and the discussion is only as to whether the conditions are favourable. And one of the conditions to be considered is whether the dead of night is likely to be dark or bright.

Most of these men are known to the police, and many of them are "under observation." Millsom and Fowler were being watched by special instructions from Scotland Yard all through January and right up to the time they committed the burglary and murder at Muswell Hill. The burglars knew this so well that after the crime they hid in Highgate Wood until between five and six in the morning, and then started to walk home, thinking, in the words of Millsom's confession, "that at that time the police would be fairly scarce."

Then they walked from Muswell Hill through Kilburn to North Kensington, with the proceeds of the crime upon them.

Fowler's clothes were covered with blood-stains. To hide them he wore Millsom's brown overcoat. Though they were watched and wanted men, they walked through London reeking from their crime without attracting attention, because they had timed their return for the quietest part of the night.

The early hours from two to four are the burglar's hours for business; the hour for the walk home is later, that criminals returning from work may be mistaken for honest men going to it.

But there is romance in the dead of night, and the mystery of the world's work as well as of dark deeds.

London, the mighty city, slumbers not nor sleeps. In the darkest hours of the night the work is going forward for the needs of the great city, that will presently wake to another day of life.

The side streets leading to the great markets are blocked with a great traffic of laden vans. The news of the world is being prepared in great printing offices for the million eyes as yet closed in sleep. Through the quiet wards of the great hospitals the sisters of suffering move gently from bed to bed, tending the maimed and sick.

The refreshment houses of the night-workers are open, and between four and five o'clock many of them are packed with breakfasting guests. Down by the dock gates a great crowd of men has gathered long before the grey dawn throws their anxious and often careworn faces into relief. These men have waited, many of them, through the dead of night to be nearest to the great gates when they open, and the foremen come to choose the hands that are needed for the unloading of the ships.

And there among the crowd waiting, some of them in the last despair for a day's work, you may find many a mystery. All the men who wait in dumb patience through the long hours for the dock gates to open are not of the labouring class. The wreckage drifts to the dock gates for a job, because it is the great market for unskilled labour.

I have seen in the crowd army men, 'varsity men, City men, actors, stockbrokers, and once a clergyman. To the dock gates there came a year or two back, day after day, a baronet. He was ill-clad, hungry, and broken-hearted. He got a job at last, only to be sent away before he had done a couple of hours' work, because he was too weak for the task he had undertaken in his last desperate strait.

But as the dead of night yields to the dawn, there are brighter scenes to look upon than the listless, anxious-eyed crowd at the dock gates and the wharves of the great river of wealth.

Soon after four, in many a little side street, the professional caller goes his round to rouse the sleepers who must be early astir, and by five there is a plentiful sprinkling of healthy-looking, clean-faced, stalwart men tramping along steadily, pipe in mouth and cloth-wrapped dinner in hand, wending their way to the labour of the day.

The trains have begun to discharge their human freight. Over the bridges pours a steady stream of humanity, the steam whistles sound shrilly on the morning air, the warning bells of the factories clang noisily. The rest of the night is over, the work of the day has begun, the evil-doer has slunk away into the darkness, and the honest breadwinners go cheerfully to their work, looking the whole world in the face.

CHAPTER XXIV
THE UNDIVULGED SECRET

A lie, then eternity—A promise made to the dying—Insurance money tempts them—"Have not betrayed"—The innocent who die for the guilty—The girl who lives as a boy

AS the world knows nothing of its greatest men, so the world knows nothing of its greatest mysteries. No hint or rumour of them ever reaches the public ear. There are strange things happening every day in this vast, mysterious world that we call London of which no word will ever be spoken. One or two human beings will know the secret, but it will remain hidden away in their hearts to the end.

Sometimes from the lips of a dying man or woman comes a confession that startles and shocks the few interested relatives gathered round the bedside. Sometimes even in these deathbed revelations—the last despairing effort of the burthened conscience to find relief while still a flicker of life remains—there is still a reticence and a reservation. The nearest and dearest are not trusted with the secret, even in that supreme hour. The full confession is made only to the priest, upon whose lips is the seal of silence.

The knowledge that in death there is often this desire to clear the conscience by a confession, has caused many people to believe that mysteries which to the world still remain unfathomed have been revealed by criminals dying on the scaffold. There are people who still remember the confession Neill Cream made with the rope round his neck.

"I am Jack the ————-" he gasped, and then his lips closed in the eternal silence. This confession, like others of a similar kind, has been generally accepted as a desperate attempt to prolong life. The wretched man imagined that by making this statement his execution might be stayed in order that his story might be inquired into, for he knew that all the world was eager to have that mystery of mysteries cleared up. But there were facts known to those on the scaffold which stamped the statement as a lie—a lie uttered on the brink of eternity.

In the dead of night, in the ward of one of our great hospitals, some time ago, the nurse in charge was sitting by the stove at the end of the room when she heard a faint cry from one of the beds.

She went at once, and found that one of the patients, a man of fifty who was not expected to live, had taken a sudden turn for the worse. She saw that the man was dying, and was about to summon the doctor on night-duty when the dying man grasped her hand.

"Don't go, for God's sake!" he gasped. "Listen!—I'm dying—I want to tell you something—something that when I am gone you will keep as a sacred secret."

The nurse, somewhat alarmed by the man's manner, gave the promise. She bent down to hear what he had to say. Then with a white face she went hurriedly to the telephone and called to the doctor.

The man died shortly afterwards. He died and left the nurse in possession of a secret which she would have given a great deal never to have heard. She gave a solemn promise to a dying man not to reveal it, and yet she has confessed that the temptation to do so is great. She asserts that if she opened her lips a mystery which startled London, and which is still unsolved, would be a mystery no more. But the dying man gave her his confession as the professional nurse by his bedside and under an oath of secrecy, and she holds that she is bound by it. There is one person in the world who knows the secret of that mystery—and only one. And she will probably carry it with her to the grave.

There is many a mystery, of which no word has ever been breathed abroad, hidden away under the marble tombs and flower-decked graves of our great cemeteries.

It has happened that a belated traveller, passing the gates of a cemetery in the hours of darkness, has been startled to see among the distant tombs dim lanterns moving here and there. He has probably hurried away, for not many of us are brave enough to overcome the dread of watching a city of the dead after nightfall.

But he has only seen the preparations for the carrying out of the Home Secretary's order for exhumation. An unsuspected crime is believed to have been hidden away in the graveyard.

Something has come to light which has aroused suspicion, and the proverb that "Murder will out" is about to be justified again.

But there are mysteries of crime which lie in the cemeteries never to be brought to the light of day, and there are mysteries of romance lying there unsuspected too.

The allegations in the famous Druce-Portland mystery startled England. They remain allegations, for the Home Secretary has persistently refused to allow the truth of the tomb to be laid bare. But there are empty coffins in family vaults and under splendid monuments, and there are coffins tenanted by men and women who never bore the name that is upon the coffin-plate.

The sham funeral always conceals a mystery which is not likely to be revealed, for those who have arranged it have the best of reasons for keeping lifelong silence.

The sham or substituted burial takes place, as a rule, in connection with insurance frauds.

I have given chapter and verse in a former chapter with regard to the substitution of bodies, and quoted from the evidence given before a Parliamentary Commission to prove that fraud under our present system of death certification is not only possible but quite easy of accomplishment.

Here is a case which will prove to the doubting reader how simple it is to bury a man with all formalities satisfied, while he is still alive.

A doctor had been attending a man who was seriously ill. He called one morning, found the patient apparently much worse, and told the relatives—poor people!—that he would look in again in the evening about nine o'clock.

At eight o'clock the man's wife came to the doctor's house, told him the patient had passed away, and asked for a certificate. The doctor, who expected the man to die, and had been attending him for some time, gave it.

Before the wife got home the doctor's assistant, who that evening was going the doctor's rounds for him, as he—the doctor—had a private matter which made him anxious not to leave his home, called on the patient, whose name was on the list he had copied from the doctor's visiting-book.

He found the man much better and sitting up in bed chatting with his brother, who was drinking his health from a newly-opened bottle of whisky. This accidental visit of the assistant spoilt a neatly-arranged scheme of fraud.

The patient was insured for £100. Shortly after the doctor's visit he took a remarkable turn for the better, and towards evening was on the road to recovery. The crisis had passed, and he was out of danger.

The husband's brother came in, and suggested to the man and his wife that it would be a pity to lose the £100 that would have come to the family if the patient had died. So the wife went out and got the certificate.

These facts are in the Report of the Commission. The doctor who attended the case told the story himself in the course of his evidence.

It was some time afterwards that the plan for the false burial was discovered. The money for it was to be drawn from the burial club on the doctor's certificate. The relatives had managed to get possession of a shell. This was to be filled with stones and bricks, securely wrapped up to prevent their moving, and packed in a sack to represent the man's weight.

The shell was to be closed, and then, "in consequence of a dispute with the first undertaker," the order for the coffin and the interment was to be given to another undertaker.

There was no reason he should refuse the business. The production of the doctor's certificate would justify him in taking the order and concluding the arrangements.

There are coffins in the London cemeteries which contain no bodies. Over some of the graves there are memorial stones, and, as in Wilkie Collins' famous story, "The Woman in White," it sometimes happens that the "dead person" goes to the cemetery and reads the touching tribute to his or her virtues.

It may even be—I have heard the story told—that the dear departed will go to the cemetery once a year and lay a memorial wreath upon her own grave.

These are the mysteries of the dead. The mysteries of the living are hidden away, sometimes in their own hearts, sometimes in the keeping of the family solicitor, who has many a startling romance locked away in the safes and tin boxes that line the walls of his quiet office.

I sat the other day in the private office of a famous solicitor who is the confidant of the secrets of many of our titled families, and of some of the most prominent members of the Smart Set.

As I chatted pleasantly with the famous lawyer, I could not help thinking what a marvellous series of "Mysteries of modern London" he could write if he were not, by reason of his office and his own high sense of personal honour, bound to preserve silence.

In the quiet, old-fashioned little room in which I sat, looking out upon an ancient burial ground, some of the most sensational stories of the day have been told, and, by the skill of the diplomatic solicitor, brought to a satisfactory last chapter, and then consigned to the oblivion of the locked safe, of which he alone carries the key.

For most of the mysteries that have been brought to this cosy little room have been settled there. They have not had to endure the glare of the Law Courts and the fierce publicity of the Press. Had they done so the world would have had some startling sensations, which would have put many that are thrillingly headlined by the popular Press far back into the shade.

It is not often in this country that we have the mystery of the concealed identity in the criminal dock. No advocate rises at the Old Bailey and endeavours to influence a jury by hinting that the prisoner on trial for his life is the son of some great personage. "If you knew who I was," exclaimed Prado, "you would be astounded," and his advocate repeated his words.

We have no guilty wretches posing in the dock and pretending that by their silence they are screening a name which is dearer to them than life. Something of that kind was, it is true, attempted by Mrs. Pearcy (Mary Eleanor Wheeler), the murderess of Mrs. Hogg and her child, who arranged that after her death an advertisement should be inserted in all the principal Madrid papers.

The advertisement duly appeared:

"M. E. C. P. Last wish of M. E. W. Have not betrayed."

The story of the murder of Mrs. Hogg was only half told. Mrs. Pearcy practically acknowledged her guilt when she said that her sentence was just; but there was always an unfathomed mystery in the case which was intensified by the last request of the woman on the brink of eternity, that someone in a foreign land should be notified that she had "not betrayed."

Yet innocent persons have suffered for others and have not betrayed. An innocent man has stood in the shadow of the scaffold and refused to say the words which would have cleared him, because they would have imperilled the life of one whom he was determined not to betray.

Innocent men and innocent women have confessed to crimes and paid the penalty. The story told by the French novelist of the man in the last stage of consumption who confessed to a murder by arrangement with the relatives of the real murderer has its counterpart in fact. The man, who proved that truth is stranger than fiction, feared a public trial. He committed suicide, and left a confession behind him which tallied with all the ascertained facts. His confession could well bear the impress of truth, for the details were communicated to him by the actual author of the crime. The man took the eternal shame upon himself for a sum of money assured to those who, had he died of the disease that must soon have been fatal, would have been left in the direst poverty. It was not until some years after the suicide of the supposed murderer that suspicion was aroused as to the genuineness of the confession by certain circumstances which came accidentally to the knowledge of a retired police-officer. And then it was useless to move further in the matter. To obtain the conviction of another man would, in the circumstances, have been almost impossible.

In the old days physical torture wrung a false confession of guilt from hundreds of men and women. To-day it is mental torture that now and again causes an innocent person to plead guilty to crimes that can be purged with imprisonment, but more frequently there is a solid and substantial benefit as the temptation.

Occasionally, when in some famous case of elaborate fraud there is a suspicion that the person arrested is a man of good family fallen into evil ways, there is a hint in the Press of the mystery of identity. But it is rarely more than a hint. No one knows the truth but the unhappy man himself and his still unhappier relatives, who throughout the trial are in terror lest the accused should, in a moment of weakness, betray himself, and fix the shame of his evil-doings upon the name they bear.

But, as a rule, the well-born man who has fallen low respects his family, and the mystery of the identity of many a criminal who passes from the dock to the convict gaol has been as well preserved, as far as the great public are concerned, as the identity of the Man in the Iron Mask.

One reads old stories of women who all their lives have passed without suspicion as men, and accepts them as possible in the past. But sometimes the world is startled by the discovery that this mystery of sex is still maintained by women even in the lowlier walks of life, where one would think romance of the kind would have no place.

Not long since a working-man, grey-haired and wrinkled, came before a London magistrate, and was proved to be a woman. She had passed as a man and laboured as a man for nearly forty years, and no one had suspected the truth.

In some cases, for good and sufficient reasons, this form of fraud—for in a sense it is fraud—is aided and abetted by relatives, who keep the secret to the end.

One has only to remember that large sums of money and vast estates pass away from families in default of an heir male to understand how sometimes the girl-child is dressed and brought up as a "boy" from the earliest period.

The fraud *must* sooner or later be found out, you would think. But with money to back it up there is no absolute reason that it should be.

Many of these men-women have been married to "wives," and the wife has kept the secret. There are a dozen cases known and authenticated to prove it.

In most instances the secret has been discovered or confessed at last. But there are some cases in which the secret is kept undivulged through life and passed on to the eternal silence of the grave.